To Mary Ann

From Tim, Tabitha

& Don.

The Missionary Wife
and Her Work

The Missionary Wife and Her Work

BY
JOY TURNER TUGGY

MOODY PRESS
CHICAGO

To
my mother,
my mother-in-law,
and
my husband,
who, under God, have taught me
the importance of these things;
and
to the many missionary mothers and children
whose assistance has made this study possible.

CONTENTS

Chapter   Page

Introduction 9

1. Her Devotional Life 13

2. Her Husband 43

3. Her Children 52

4. Her Home 97

5. Her Missionary Work 124

6. Her Fellow Missionaries 157

7. Her Home Church 168

8. Mature Reflections 182

9. Her Ministry in Perspective 186

INTRODUCTION

W HOLE VOLUMES have been written on the stresses in the life of the missionary: the interruptions, the pressures from without and from within, the relentless drive of duties, the constant sense of responsibility, the necessity of accomplishing what is set before him in the face of insufficient funds, help, and even physical strength.

But among missionaries there is a group which is, in a sense, subject to special strains—mothers. The missionary mother shares equally with her husband in the call to service in a foreign land. Sensing keenly the need of the people to whom they minister, deeply conscious of a Christian indebtedness to minister Christ to them, she also is aware of a basic personal responsibility before God which she is in danger of neglecting—her children. Continued neglect of this responsibility will almost certainly mean the ultimate undermining of what she and her husband can do as missionaries.

Her conflict can be considerable. Her sense of frustration, of limitation, of failure can, for a time, bring all useful, joyful service to a standstill.

Mission boards recognize this situation. In the notes of the EFMA Executives' Retreat of 1959 is the following observation:

> Many missionary parents and mission executives sometimes find themselves involved in a conflict between discharging their God-given responsibilities to the chil-

9

dren and their equally God-given responsibilities to further the evangelization of the world.[1]

It should be said that to a certain degree the boards are patient and cooperative with a "part-time missionary" mother. Still, in a very real sense, it is a problem to which the woman herself, subject to her husband and to the Lord, must find the solution.

Simply being married does not necessarily distract a woman from the Lord's service, particularly in missionary work. Rather, the joining of two lives under God in the intimate union of marriage provides enhanced possibilities for service, both public and private.

It is when the Lord gives children that a woman finds her freedom to serve seriously curtailed by seemingly mundane activities. Then she is seized with a baffling sense of limitation, a fear of neglecting what she feels to be her whole life-work. If a woman's sights are not adjusted and her spiritual perception clarified, she may begin to feel that she is being forced into disobedience to the Lord's will for her life.

This is not an extreme statement. Most mission fields can testify to the heartbreak of missionary children who have been sacrificed to "the Lord's work" and who will never enter into the heritage of glad, fruitful service which could have been theirs.

Some have become embittered and have turned against the things of the Lord. For these there is no excuse. Whether their parents were right or wrong, the Lord Himself did not fail them. It is to Him that they are personally responsible. He has ways of blessing and triumph in which He will lead any missionary child, regardless of his parents' mistakes.

Still, missionary parents do need to evaluate very seriously their responsibility before God for their children. Their loss is a very personal one, but it is more than personal.

---

[1]*Reports and Findings,* Vol. VIII, Mission Executives' Retreat (Evangelical Foreign Missions Association, 1405 G St., N.W. Washington D. C., Sept. 28-Oct. 2, 1959), p. 7.

There is plenty of evidence to support the fact that the children of missionaries are not only the best source of future missionary recruits, but also that they make the best missionaries. It is also sadly true that some missionary children have apparently been turned aside from the things of God and from considering missionary service by failure on the part of their parents and/or their missionary society to provide proper home life, or social and educational opportunities.[2]

The problem, then, is a complicated one, due to the various areas of stress and especially to the sense of duty to two responsibilities which are equally God-given but often in apparent conflict.

In approaching the problem, we will first seek to ascertain what a woman's primary responsibilities are before God, as set forth in Scripture.

Next, we will consider the multiple demands made upon her, seeking, if possible, to strip each to its essentials, and to give practical solutions that women on the mission field have found helpful. To this end, we have sought and obtained the cooperation of eighty-nine missionary mothers on thirty-five different missionary fields. Their answers to questionnaires and letters have made unmistakably clear the fact that while the problem is present and unavoidable, it is, under God, capable of solution.

Particular attention will be given to the essential duties of motherhood, as this is the area which distinguishes the missionary mother from all other missionaries. Here twelve children of missionaries have contributed valuable assistance by giving, in retrospect, an evaluation of their experience and observation.

Third, search will be made for the secret of spiritual and emotional rest which will make possible the highest efficiency in carrying out all that is laid upon the missionary mother.

---

[2]*Ibid.*

The study and evaluation of these questionnaires have been undertaken with great care. It is not a small thing that so many missionary mothers should have permitted others to look into their intimate lives. Their candid appraisal of themselves, in weakness and in strength, as the Lord has given it, has made their statements authoritative and helpful. Their cooperation in answering the questionnaires was remarkably prompt and full, and their response was so cordial as to be very encouraging. Not only that, the fact that so many found time to answer, in spite of their many duties, indicated a high degree of self-discipline and graciousness of spirit. One must honor them and trust God, with them, for increased usefulness and blessing as He controls their lives.

CHAPTER 1

HER DEVOTIONAL LIFE

I DON'T SEE how you do it all. How can you be a teacher, housekeeper, missionary, wife, mother, and registrar?" The missionary who received this letter from her sister in the homeland laughed ruefully to herself as she read the letter. Then she wrote back: "Ruthie, you have the order wrong. First I'm a Christian, then a wife, then a mother, then a missionary, and finally, what time is left, a housewife."

This true story implies conflict in the mind of the missionary concerning her various roles. Under the pressure of multiple duties clamoring for attention, many a confused missionary has found herself before the Lord seeking His thought about her daily life.

What does He consider to be of first importance?

What priorities would He set up for secondary tasks?

Are any of her responsibilities self-assumed and not God-given?

Are unnecessary, unproductive activities needlessly draining off spiritual or physical energies?

A Look at Women of the Bible

So she goes to the Word, for in the Word of God she will find instruction concerning herself as a woman, as a wife and mother, and as a servant of the Lord. What she finds in God's Word will enable her to set up some priorities for her life and will give her every reason to expect she will be able to fulfill her responsibilities successfully.

She finds in Genesis 2:18-22 that woman was created distinctly for man.

A careful study of the Old Testament reveals women whose lives helped (like Ruth) or hindered (like Jezebel) their husbands, as well as women whose spiritual ideals blessed (like Hannah) or marred (like Rebekah) their children. We find children who did not walk after their fathers' holy paths, like the sons of Eli and Samuel. It is not for us to blame, but all mothers would be wise to take warning, for in the historical accounts of the kings of Judah is found an oft-repeated reminder: "And the name of his mother was . . ."

Even in Old Testament times there were women peculiarly in the Lord's work, such as Deborah (Judges 4:4) and Huldah the prophetess (II Chron. 34:22). These were married women.

The Old Testament law concerning a woman's vow should also be considered in this study (Num. 30:3). A woman's vow was always made under the authority of her father or her husband, who could annul it on the spot or cause it to stand.

The book of Psalms has several noteworthy passages: Psalm 45, which speaks of the "king's daughter" as "all glorious" (v. 13), exhorts her (vv.10-11) to forget her own people and her father's house and to cleave to her husband, "for he is thy lord; and reverence thou him." This it couples with future blessing and fruitfulness. "Instead of thy fathers shall be thy children, whom thou shalt make princes in all the earth" (v. 16).

We also read in the book of Psalms: "The Lord giveth the word: the women that publish the tidings are a great host" (68:11). From this verse it could be deduced that missionary women are not new.

Proverbs has numerous references to women. A prudent wife is from the Lord (19:14). "A worthy woman is the crown of her husband" (12:4). Chapter 31 outlines the various skills of such a woman and her qualities of thrift, industry, faithfulness, business acumen, integrity, organizational ability, kindness, and generosity, as well as the position of honor in which she is held.

In the prophets, woman is used as a picture of either faithfulness or unfaithfulness, but chiefly as the representation of one whom the Lord desires to be wholly, intimately, unswervingly His own, whether she is spoken of literally or figuratively. The Lord Jesus reiterated the teaching of Genesis (Matt. 19:4-6, Mark 10:6-11) and strengthened it, saying, "What therefore *God* hath joined, let not man put asunder." Thus Jesus gave to marriage a definite place of priority over other interests and emphasized its permanency in human life.

However, He also said, "If any man cometh unto me, and hateth not his own father, and mother, and wife, and children, and brethren, and sisters, yea, and his own life also, he cannot be my disciple" (Luke 14:26; cf Luke 18:29), showing clearly that neither marriage nor any other human relationship or responsibility is *first* in the Lord's sight.

In both the Gospels and the book of Acts you read of many godly women who ministered to the Lord and to His people of their substance. To some of them He revealed deep truths (John 4:24; 11:25). There are the mothers whose sons became the Timothy and the John Mark whom the Lord used to bring such blessing to the church as a whole. There were wives whose lives greatly strengthened their husbands for wrongdoing (Acts 5:2) or for blessing (Acts 18:26).

Finally, in the epistles definite doctrinal teaching about married women is given to the Christian church. These passages are so clear as to afford a very real comfort and sense of direction to a confused Christian woman.

Three statements in I Corinthians 7 apply directly to this study. The first, in verses 3 to 5 ("The wife hath not power over her own body . . ."), is related to the teaching of Hebrews 13:4 that "marriage is honorable in all, and the bed undefiled . . ." (AV). It speaks of the mutual subjection of the married partners, in love and before the Lord, with their spiritual well-being dependent upon it. First Corinthians 7:34 suggests the possibility that a married woman may get her eyes on her husband and center her aims on him rather than on the Lord. More will be given of this text later. Another basic concept is presented in I Corinthians 7:39: Marriage, in God's plan, is for life. "A wife is bound for so long time as her husband liveth." This was the teaching of the Lord, as was mentioned previously.

Then I Corinthians 11 and 14 introduce a subject beautifully expounded in Ephesians 5 (see also Col. 3:15), in which the wife is told to be in subjection to her own husband in everything as unto the Lord, for she is a picture of the church being subject to Christ. A helpful unity of emphasis on this responsibility of the wife is found in Ephesians 5:22, Colossians 3:18, I Peter 3:1 and 3:5. These verses speak not of the submission of one Christian to another, but of the special submission of a wife to her own husband—the God-imposed duty of a woman to acknowledge freely the lordship of her husband over her. There seems to be no way to sidestep this instruction. The godly woman will face it squarely and in glad acceptance of it will find undreamed-of freedom to serve the Lord she loves.

The passage closes with the words "Let the wife see that she fear her husband" (Eph. 5:33). This term "fear" leads to I Peter 3, where Peter makes God's ideal of beauty a very concrete thing: ". . . let it be the hidden man of the heart, in the incorruptible apparel of a meek and quiet spirit, which is in the sight of God of great price." Peter reminds women that they are only fitting into the pattern of holy women of old who hoped in God, being in subjection to their own husbands. In this context "fear" is used with both a positive and a negative aspect. Women are to fear their husbands (3:2, 6) in the sense of reverencing them, venerating them, treating them with deference and reverential obedience, but they are not to "be put in fear by any terror" (3:6), that is, they are not to fear the terrifying things of life.

The "studio portrait" of a truly beautiful woman is marked, then, by meekness, quietness, purity, and a deeply wrought spiritual courage. Any woman will recognize instantly that these qualities, to be in her, must be the work of God; and she will long to possess them.

In I Timothy 3:11 the Apostle Paul gives a list of qualities necessary for women who are to have special positions of service in the church. They are to be grave, not slanderers, temperate, faithful in all things.

Paul, writing to Titus, tells him (Titus 2:1,3-5) to speak "the things which befit the sound doctrine." Included among these things is instruction to the aged women to "be reverent in demeanor, not slanderers, nor enslaved to much wine, teachers of that which is good; that they may train the young women to love their husbands,

>to love their children,
>to be sober-minded,
>chaste,
>workers at home,
>kind,
>being in subjection to their own husbands,
>>that the word of God be not blasphemed."

Paul, speaking in I Timothy 5:14 of young widows who should remarry, said they should:

>"bear children,
>rule the household,
>give no occasion to the adversary for reviling."

There is no need to go into the controversial aspects of I Corinthians 11 and 14, and I Timothy 2. It is true that Paul never allowed a woman to teach in the church (I Tim. 2:12). For the purposes of this study, we find in Paul's writings ample scope for a woman's teaching ministry. (Cf Titus 2:3-4; I Timothy 5:14; 2:15, and the implications of II Timothy 1:5 with 3:15). And from the book of Acts we learn that in the time of Paul there were women with the ability to expound the Scriptures and to prophesy (cf. Acts 18:26; 21:9). But all of woman's ministry was to be carried on with an attitude which evidenced "subjection," which has already been considered.

It should be observed, perhaps, that both I Corinthians 14 and I Timothy 2 emphasize silence in a *learning* situation. The practicality of this becomes completely understandable in regions where custom and culture do not impose a courteous, attentive silence upon a group of listeners. Often it is the women who want to gabble. Missionary mothers do well to learn to restrain themselves and their children, and to exert a loving influence upon the ladies of the congregations to obey these commands literally.

In I Timothy 2:9-10 women are told to dress modestly and to adorn themselves with an ornament which is very tangible —"good works." Surely this is her linen robe (Rev. 19:8), finely wrought by the indwelling, outworking Spirit of God in her life.

The marriage relationship is put into perspective in I Corinthians 7:29-31: "The time is shortened, that henceforth both those that have wives may be as though they had none; . . . and those that buy as though they possessed not; and those that use the world, as not using it to the full: for the fashion of this world passeth away."

There is only one earthly relationship that will pass over integrally into eternal life. It is the personal relationship to the Lord Jesus. The love of husband and wife, of mother and child, of dear ones in Christ, will be sweetened and deepened and purified, but also changed. On the other hand, He Who is the full portion of the Christian now will continue to be that in eternity; and a Christian woman's love for Him will be immeasurably enriched as she can be conscious at last of pleasing Him utterly.

For this reason, the missionary mother will conclude that her first and most important relationship is her personal relationship to her Lord. From this relationship all others stem as the Lord gives them, and her effectiveness in them depends entirely on how closely she is walking with Him. Her heart is His. She must guard it with all diligence, for out of it are the issues of life. Then by the grace of God, she *and* her husband

and her children *and* the native Christians of the land where they have labored will all be in the presence of the Lord forever, where these secondary relationships will be swallowed up in the far richer, sweeter union of all with Christ.

ONE SUPREME COMMITMENT

A missionary mother can be relieved of all her responsibilities but one. Her husband may be taken from her, or her children removed by the hand of the Lord, but while life lasts, she is a Christian. This expresses a committal to Christ which is lasting, unconditional, and prior to all other considerations. This is the foundation upon which her life is ordered; it is the beam by which her decisions are guided; it is the deep wellspring of her life.

In a sense, she is just an ordinary Christian, and the laws of life and spiritual health apply to her as to any other Christian. They are, however, important to her in a special sense. She has gone out as a representative of her Lord before a people who know Him not. Further, the effectiveness of her husband's ministry and the pattern for her children's lives are greatly dependent upon the quality of her spiritual life and its outworking in her daily walk.

Problems in Her Devotional Life

With so much at stake, it becomes necessary to consider the forces that work against her—and their manifestations are numerous.

First, she experiences the ordinary interruptions of any housewife: the children that need attention at just the wrong time; the emergencies that are endemic to a household; the unexpected visitors that stay on and on and on.

Then there are the frustrations that set her on edge: the carefully made plans so suddenly upset; the frustration of "not quite enough" with which to make ends meet; the constant battle against impatience (or perhaps anger) with servants and children, or even with fellow workers who may not be particularly compatible.

Physically, she may be affected, consciously or unconsciously, by the climate of the country she is working in. For instance, if she is sent to a tropical country, she will need to go through a period of adjustment to tropical conditions. Later, after many years of arduous work in a tropical climate, she may become very exhausted. And no matter what climate she works in, she will experience daily weariness under heavy burdens. These are a few of the physical problems which may subtly affect her spiritual health.

She may have strong emotional reactions—sometimes to long-continued irritation, and at other times because of sudden provocation. Such reactions will be tempered by the odd ebb and flow of feeling most women are subject to in greater or lesser degree. Because her emotions are likely to express themselves in action, they must be carefully evaluated and brought under control.

The missionary wife also bears spiritual burdens. These can begin with an overwhelming sense of personal incapacity and spiritual lack. Add to this a deep sense of the need of those about her, complicated, probably, by the realization that very little growth in grace is being manifested in their lives, and you find you have every necessary ingredient for weariness in well-doing and utter discouragement.

To a certain extent these problems are common to all Christians. But the missionary mother has a special sphere of responsibility, and she must learn the secret of a steady Christian walk. Her personal testimony and her ministry in the lives of others demand that the Lord work in her a real spiritual and emotional stability. She must become in very truth "a weaned child," finding in her God the fulfillment of her every need and the solution to her every problem. She must steadfastly keep her eyes fixed upon the unchanging God.

Without a proper devotional life, anyone's Christian life will lack constancy and be practically devoid of power. And many a missionary is highly disturbed because it is hard for him to get time alone with the Lord. But for the missionary mother the difficulties are multiplied. If she gets up early in the morning, so do the children. If she sets aside a time after breakfast, it is hard to get the day's activities for her children or the servants under way. If she decides to have her devotions at night so she will not be interrupted, she is often too tired to pray sensibly or to benefit properly from any but the most relaxed reading of the Word.

One mother who had six children and had served many, many years on the field wrote: "I have often envied the father the privilege of slipping away for a quiet time without family responsibilities, but perhaps I have not availed myself of the early hours when I might have done so too."

Another mother of four (all missionaries), a veteran of well over fifty years' service on the field, said gently: "Daddy never could understand why I couldn't drop everything and have my quiet time early in the morning as he did."

Rosalind Goforth, in her book *Climbing*, wryly recounts an experience that has certainly aroused deep sympathy in other missionary mothers:

> . . . On one occasion, this dear woman, who had no children, told me that I could never have the peace and joy I longed for unless I rose early and spent one to two hours with the Lord in prayer and Bible Study.
>
> I longed intensely for God's best—for all He could give me, not only to help me to live the true, Christian life but also for peace and rest of soul. So I determined to do what Mrs. S. had advised.
>
> The following morning, about half past five o'clock, I slipped as noiselessly as possible out of bed. (My husband had already gone to his study.) I had taken only a step or two when first one and then another little head bobbed up; then came calls of "Mother, is it time to get up?"
>
> "Hush, hush, no, no," I whispered as I went back; but

too late: baby had wakened! So, of course, the morning circus began an hour too soon.

But I did not give up easily. Morning after morning I tried rising early for the morning watch, but always with the same result. So I went back to the old way of just praying quietly—too often just sleeping! Oh, how I envied my husband, who could have an hour or more of uninterrupted Bible study; but I could not. This led me to form the habit of memorizing Scripture, which became an untold blessing to me. I took advantage of odd opportunities on cart, train, or when dressing, always to have a Bible or Testament at hand so that in the early mornings I could recall precious promises and passages of Scripture.[1]

THE QUIET TIME—A NECESSITY

The point is that none of these difficulties rules out the basic fact that the missionary mother *must* meet her Lord daily, face to face, and *must* have quiet, deep intercourse with Him. The reason is simple: apart from Him, she has no life; and she dares not face missionary motherhood without a constantly abundant and outgoing life.

Dr. T. Stanley Soltau, of Korea, wrote this about missionary life:

> . . . the foreign missionary is facing . . . a situation that can be changed only by a miracle-working God. It is a situation which he can face year after year without discouragement and sense of defeat only as the same omnipotent God works a miracle in his heart and life and causes him to enjoy a joyous confidence and a buoyancy of spirit that is unexplainable from natural causes and is a direct result of the working of the Holy Spirit in his own life day after day.
>
> All these circumstances and experiences, then, make it essential that the missionary learn, if he does not already know, how to seek and to receive new enduements

---

[1]Rosalind Goforth, *Climbing* (Chicago: Moody Press), p. 76.

of divine power, wisdom, tact, and courage that will re-
plenish and refurbish his spiritual resources, enabling
him to go on . . . The secrets of power on the foreign
mission field are exactly the same as those in the home-
lands. They perhaps become more easily understood
because of the absolute necessity of making use of them
daily in view of the absence of any of the helpful influences and spiritual "props" which are so common and so
accessible at home.[2]

These things being so, the problem resolves itself into the
practical question, "What time of day can I keep relatively
free of interruption for a quiet time apart with the Lord?" It
is a question that must be studied by the individual, but with
God's help and direction the missionary mother can find a
solution. She will need a certain consecrated stubbornness
and considerable flexibility in response to the demands of
other people, but the desires of the heart that "panteth after
the water brooks" will not be denied. The Lord will always
enable a woman to meet Him if she asks His help.

In the everyday situation in which a missionary mother
finds herself, she must consider these controlling factors: the
age of the children, the amount and quality of servant help,
the family schedule, her missionary duties, and her own health.

Of the more than one hundred mothers who responded to
my questionnaire, the great majority have found getting a
daily quiet time a very real problem—so much so that one
commented: "My greatest lack during the first term was
fitting in an uninterrupted quiet time when the children were
babies." Another mother asked if she had not found some solution to this problem of many interruptions, wrote, "No, because at other times I would be disturbed even more." A typical mother commented, "There is no answer, and the Lord
understands."

Only eight felt they had found a time when they would be

---

[2]T. Stanley Soltau, *Facing the Field* (Grand Rapids: Baker Book House,
1959), p. 124.

disturbed rarely, and it was interesting to discover that the time elected by these ranged from very early in the morning all through the day to very late at night. The after-breakfast hours were chosen by women whose families all left for work and school and who were apparently in more isolated homes and a more modern situation. The children's nap hours were clearly only a temporary solution. Children take naps for only a few years.

The late night hours would seem to be an almost perfect solution, but most women are so tired by nighttime that prayer —especially intercessory prayer—becomes sheer effort. One woman said, "If not in the morning, then never." But for several women the luxury of a quiet time that is all one's own, even though it be occasionally interrupted, provides a sense of relaxation and restfulness which rather quickens their minds. "I can think and concentrate better in the evening after all is quiet," said one. Another said, "After the children are in bed there are few interruptions; mornings are too busy."

A mother of three wrote:

> This for me, as well as many missionary mothers, was a problem. When a baby is small there is usually time in the early morning after she or he was fed. When they get to the place of an afternoon nap only, I found that just after lunch was a good time. Morning is definitely the best time, but the Africans are at your door at daybreak, so it means arising very early.

Another wrote briefly:

> I prefer early morning, though that is not always possible with "small fry" who seem to waken as soon as one stirs. My husband and I have found that a period taken right after rest hour is a very profitable practice.

Still another said:

> I remember when our first one was little and used to interrupt my attempts at devotions, that I often felt impatient and disturbed about it. But I came to realize that

this attitude was wrong, and then endeavored to find another quiet time during the day. It is not an easily solved problem. But even the quiet time before breakfast is no guarantee for ability to meet every crisis; therefore the necessity of a moment-by-moment walk with God.

The morning hour is the most desirable in the opinion of the majority, but one observation constantly recurred: When the children are small, they make it very difficult for their mother to have a quiet time unless she can manage to awaken early without disturbing them. When the family lives in cramped quarters, this is difficult. One mother told of lying awake in bed in the early morning, praying quietly so the children would not realize she was awake. This was a partial solution but was not entirely satisfactory because there was always the possibility of going back to sleep.

One mother asks the Lord to awaken her during the night for quiet time. She then has an uninterrupted hour with Him, after which she goes back to finish her night's sleep. Another mother told of having practiced this at a certain period in her ministry. The trouble is that many mothers, for the sake of their physical well-being, cannot afford to curtail their hours of sleep.

A mother of six children under eleven years of age wrote as follows:

> I used to find physical weariness, getting up with children, etc., made me too sleepy to get anything from my quiet time. Now I find a cup of coffee a tremendous help to making quiet time worthwhile. I find it easier to rise before the interruptions.

Other partial solutions are equally practical, especially as supplements to the quiet time.

> Talk to the Lord as you do housework—as you iron, wash dishes, and so on—have a Bible ready in the different rooms so all you need is a few minutes at various times throughout the day to read a portion of God's

Word. All day long—whenever you can—keep snatching moments to meet Him. This keeps your heart in tune with Him and others.

One missionary who has older children and well-trained servants wrote that she and her husband have their quiet time "before getting dressed in the morning. Because we aren't dressed, we aren't 'available' and the children know that we are not to be disturbed." Another mother wrote along this same line:

> We are rarely interrupted because we usually have our quiet time before activity begins. We began this when the children were small; therefore they respect this time, and we encourage them to follow the same rule.
>
> The "problem" comes when the children are small. (They *must* be taught to be quiet whenever you spend time alone with the Lord.) Often I have spent afternoons reading the Word and praying. The children informed all callers, unless it was pertinent, that I was not to be disturbed, and followed the same procedure for their daddy.

The words "problem" and "frustration" were used oftener by the mothers in discussing their quiet time in the questionnaire responses than in discussing any other matter. The primary reason appears to be that most mothers felt they must leave themselves open to interruptions. That is, they made themselves available to others. One woman wrote: "No. We live with 200-400 students who always have problems." At least twelve others simply stated that they saw no solution without taking drastic or undesirable steps. One mother expressed the opinion of many others in this way:

> Being bound to a special hour of the day causes frustration when it's interrupted. If we take the interruptions as from Him and pray as we go, then read later, we have the victory.

Another suggested that when a mother is called from her quiet time, she should meet the interruptions in a relaxed spirit, deal with the problem, and return to Bible reading or prayer.

The interruptions come to a mother through her children, through the people among whom she and her husband minister, and through emergencies. Regarding the first two, she can, after studying the problem, train the people concerned until interruptions are cut to a minimum. Such training should be done patiently and lovingly. A sharp reproof to a houseboy for having interrupted his mistress' quiet time is hardly likely to teach him how a Christian is to act when irritated.

A second cause of frustration was stated clearly by a few and implied by many. They desired to spend more time with the Lord than they seemed to be able to set apart; consequently they felt themselves to be failing to that extent. Different mothers had varying reactions, according to their background and experience, but the degree of frustration appeared to be closely related to the degree of their acceptance of the situation. A cross section of feeling might be represented by the following excerpts from several questionnaires:

> Before marriage and children, in the morning I had up to an hour. Now I am irregular up to one-half hour. In many ways I feel I've lost out in not having the quiet time.
>
> It is a proven fact that the more time we spend with the Lord just listening to Him, the greater will be our effectiveness for Him. I am guilty of not spending long enough time with Him, except in emergency! A half hour is the limit, usually.

Referring to finding a solution to this problem, one mother who normally has the same half-hour quiet time as the other two, said, "No, I did not, except that the communion continued all day with the Lord."

One mother wrote so helpfully about this that we shall quote her at length.

> As for the quiet time, I would find it very difficult to stipulate how much time should be spent, but I do think the mental attitude with which one wakens and begins her day is very important. Just to say, "Good morning, Lord. Here I am in your hands again today. Help me to use my time wisely. Take control of my mind and will so that I may make the right decisions today . . ." and then continue the prayer over the cookstove or over the sink. . . . Of course I'm speaking only of when it's really impossible to be alone for a quiet time with the Word. I wouldn't say that the days I haven't had a quiet time haven't been blessed. The Lord looks on the heart and not on what we *do*. But I would say that when I have begun a day only with the thought of all that has to be done and have spent every conscious moment planning or doing and haven't had a time of definitely committing the day to the Lord, the day has been frustrating. Of course, I don't minimize the value of time spent in the Word and on the knees.

It should be pointed out that as children grow up, the mother finds these problems dissipating. Also, with the experience of the Lord's goodness and mercy, the mothers appear to relax more, resting on the fact that the Lord meets them, rather than worrying about ineffectual efforts to meet Him. Several older women mentioned this.

> No, no solution, but it can't be helped and is much improved the longer we're here.
>
> Since the babies started coming, a quiet time before breakfast has been an impossibility. But for more than a year now, I have been able to return to this time. It is generally about one-half hour, and is a real help and preparation for the day.
>
> Many mothers get frustrated on this point. When children are small you can't stick to a set time. As one

young mother put it, "I have my devotions as soon as I can!" And that's what I did. If the children didn't wake before I did, I could have it in early morning. Other times during the night while feeding the baby, or praying during hours when you're awake at night. Otherwise, as soon as the children are down for a nap or out to play— the first quiet moment. And other times it was after they'd gone to bed at night. Now I find I can have my quiet time after they've all gone to school and it's quiet.

THE QUIET TIME—ITS PURPOSE

A word about the effectiveness of this quiet time. The important thing, so many emphasized, is not the time spent but rather whether actual contact has been made with the Lord. One mother of four young children wrote: "If I manage to get up well ahead of my family, I'm not disturbed . . . I don't feel the amount of time spent in my quiet time is the thing, but rather if I am drawing near with just my lips or with my heart."

"How long should I read?" a Bible student asked.

"Read till your heart glows!" answered the teacher.

For the missionary mother this provides a simple beginning. Her soul must be hungry and what she reads must be practical in the sense that she will continue to feed upon it through the day. Some mothers ask the Lord daily for a special portion from their reading which they write on a card or paper and pin over the desk or kitchen sink for meditation and memorization. Such a portion can glorify a difficult day.

The habit of memorization of Scripture has shown its value in the joy and comfort brought to a mother during times of need when in spite of being deprived of her normal quiet time, her soul has been nourished and restored as she meditated while she went about her duties. "Let the Word of Christ dwell in you richly . . ." is a practical command, and a mother's heart thus enriched is guided into precious truths by the Holy Spirit.

Dr. Soltau has said of missionaries:

> With the new Spirit-directed study of the Word will
> come an equally Spirit-directed application to daily life
> of the lessons learned and of the spiritual principles
> which have been made clear.[3]

Regarding prayer he writes further:

> Just as the study of, and the feeding upon, God's
> Word is a prime essential for the maintenance of spiritual
> poise and stability in the midst of circumstances which
> would naturally be very depressing and discouraging, so
> prayer also must go with it to keep the heart open to the
> Spirit's voice and warm and sensitive to His direction.
> . . . It is true here also that the necessity for it may easily
> seem more evident by reason of the desperate needs and
> the Satanic opposition which need to be met daily.[4]

Oddly enough, this matter of prayer can be decidedly frustrating to a missionary mother. She finds her heart challenged
by paragraphs like this:

> The second of these great habits is that of *secret
> prayer*. In Matthew 6:6 our Lord says, "Enter into thy
> closet"—that is the shut-in place. Eight times in that
> single verse the second personal pronoun in the singular
> number is found, teaching us the value of getting
> absolutely alone with God, looking God in the face
> before we start on the duties of the day. This habit of
> secret prayer, when joined to the other habit of daily,
> reverent Bible study, . . . clothes the disciple in the whole
> armour of God, and makes him proof against the wiles
> of the Devil.[5]

The missionary mother reads this passage with longing. Her
mind grasps the thought of *secret* prayer. She tries to locate a
"closet" for prayer. Very likely her home has no "closet" of

---

[3]*Ibid.*
[4]*Ibid.*
[5]A. T. Pierson, *Godly Self-Control* (Three Hills, Alta., Can.: Prairie
Press, n. d.), p. 100.

any kind in it, and perhaps no doors even—just curtains. She tries to think of a time when she can get "absolutely alone" with God, and she cannot isolate a waking hour when she is absolutely alone. She deliberately deprives herself of sleep to achieve this aloneness—many have—and finds that her health and her temper are seriously affected.

How can she reconcile the facts of her daily life with the commands of the Lord? Somehow she feels instinctively that prayer on her knees is of more value than prayer while she folds diapers; that prayer in private is worth more than prayer while she sweeps, with youngsters tumbling all about her. What can she do when she has no privacy?

She can remind herself that within her own heart she has the privacy of a secret place where only she and the Lord can enter. No matter how busy her home or its activities, there is still a "secret place" to which she can retire to meet the Lord, even if her children must be playing in the same room. Someone has said that it is possible to be more alone in a crowd than in a desert. In like manner a mother can be alone with the thoughts of her heart. Proverbs 14:10, for instance, tells us that "the heart knoweth its own bitterness; and a stranger doth not intermeddle with its joy," indicating that a person may have some experiences into which no one can enter—except the Lord. Fortified by her sense of the presence of the Lord, a mother can enjoy continuous fellowship with Him throughout her day, thus fulfilling the command of I Thessalonians 5:17 to "pray without ceasing."

Two letters, among others, express how the writers found rest about the matter of a quiet time by praying while they worked:

> It has always been a battle to have as much quiet time as I want and feel I should have. I have tried several solutions. . . . It seems that my quiet time invariably gets interrupted. . . . An article helped me as far as prayer time is concerned—"pray without ceasing" can become a reality as one makes beds, washes dishes,

cleans. Since I came to realize this, prayer has become less of a burden and a sweeter experience. As to the time, I find if I give myself certain limits I feel burdened and condemned when I can't meet them. But truthfully I am convicted many times for not spending enough time studying the Word.

A mother of eight wrote:

I have taken the interruptions as a test for my patience. It has taught me that I can pray and work when the pressure of duties is upon me. I used to pray only fifteen minutes or so without interruptions, but now I can take much time. An hour is soon gone before I know it.

And so the missionary mother learns to *take* time to be with her Lord, and then to live in His presence whether she is on her knees or not. She treasures the first waking moments when, except in case of an emergency, she can rejoice before the Lord in the new day that He has made. She arises already praying, and she goes on praying through the day. She will learn to go apart—whether the children or servants are around matters not—and take time to pray. For prayer can be private, even when the children are playing around the bed and occasionally stumbling over her feet. They learn to be quiet, and the mother's heart meets her God.

THE DEVOTIONAL LIFE—ITS WORTH

Perhaps we should enlarge briefly at this point on the place of prayer in her life. It has three main functions.

It is, first, her means of contact with the Lord. This is a strictly personal aspect of prayer. It involves the presentation of all her longings, her barrenness and need, her failures and sins, her rejoicings, her worship. In prayer she lays her soul bare with a complete honesty before the One who sees all things, and at the place of prayer His healing love is poured into her heart.

Second, her most important missionary work is done

through prayer. If we understood this more fully, we would pray more thoroughly. If it is true, as we say, that the solution to every problem in our missionary work lies in the hand of the God who hears prayer, it is only common sense to take those problems in detail to Him. If a missionary mother will do this, her life can be revolutionized. The Lord God can solve the individual problems of careless Christians, bickering, self-centered churches, recalcitrant unbelievers, or obstreperous, spiritually lazy missionary children.

Third, prayer is the means whereby she can enter into the common work of the church for the building up of the whole body of Christ. This is important. It is so easy for her mind to become engrossed with the problems she is facing daily that she loses all perspective of the work in which she is actually playing a tiny part—a work which is not even her own but Someone else's. Therefore she does well to make it a point to pray daily for the Lord's work in other parts of the field and elsewhere in the world. Besides giving her a part in the work on these other fields, this lifting of the eyes relaxes her involvement with her own problems and circumstances, and frees her from some of the frustrations stemming out of them. It enlarges her vision, and deepens her sense of praise and worship at what God does for others as well as herself.

Prayer calendars, prayer scrapbooks, bulletin boards with missionary pictures or letters, all are useful as guides and stimuli to prayer life. The important basic principle in praying for these others is to realize that all "temptation" is "common to man." Therefore the problems of others are similar to hers. She can, by prayer, help them bear their burdens, and so fulfill the law of Christ.

Missionaries whose lives are characterized by prayer are not at all haphazard about praying. Mrs. Howard Taylor in her biography of James O. Fraser, the missionary so signally used of God in opening the work among the Lisu, wrote of him: "More and more he was coming to depend on prayer." Then she quoted from one of his letters:

"If two of you shall agree . . ." I feel, even when praying alone, that there are two concerned in the prayer, God and myself. . . . I do not think that a petition which misses the mind of God will ever be answered (I John 5:14). Personally, I feel the need of trusting Him to lead me in prayer as well as in other matters. I find it well to preface prayer not only by meditation but by the definite request that I may be directed into the channels of prayer to which the Holy Spirit is beckoning me. I also find it helpful to make a short list, like notes prepared for a sermon, before every season of prayer. The mind needs to be guided as well as the spirit attuned. I can thus get my thoughts in order and, having prepared my prayer, can put the notes on the table or chair before me, kneel down, and get to business.[6]

Lest this should seem too businesslike and uninspired, it would be well to remember that the phrase "to labor in prayer" is not made up of idle words.

THE DEVOTIONAL LIFE—ITS OUTWORKING

But to return now to the missionary mother's daily life. The contact with the living God is spiritual, but its outreach is into all the areas of her existence. It has been well stated that the missionary's "claim to be a minister in things spiritual will find its fullest realization only in the practical outworking of a consistent and useful Christian life."[7]

Therefore, before leaving this area of our study we should consider briefly some of the more important qualities the Lord will need to work in the missionary mother, that her life may be "consistent" and "useful."

Perhaps the first should be *honesty*. Romans 12:3 teaches that we should not think more highly of ourselves than we

---

[6]Mrs. Howard Taylor, *Behind the Ranges* (Chicago: Moody Press, 1964), p. 143.

[7]Rowland Hogben, *In Training* (Chicago: Inter-Varsity Press, 1946), p. 127.

ought to think, but that we should "think soberly." A Vene-
zuelan proverb, *Del suelo para abajo no pasa,* says, freely
translated, "It won't fall any farther than the ground." Douglas
N. Sargent, in his book, *The Making of a Missionary,* writes:

> There are few more dangerous recruits than those who
> are living with a picture of themselves which is widely
> removed from reality. If Mr. Erik Routley is correct in
> suggesting that the removal of this contradiction from a
> man's life results naturally from conversion, then in a
> very real sense what such a recruit . . . requires is a more
> radical conversion. He writes, "The tension between
> what he is and what he would wish to appear to his
> neighbour is eased, and the result is a simpler, more
> direct, more clearly-drawn personality; confusion is re-
> placed by integration and harmony. Instead of being
> drawn apart by the conflicting forces of what he is and
> what he would wish to appear to be, he is now in tension
> between what he is tempted to be and what Christ can
> make him, and that tension is not grievous because, by
> the work of the Holy Spirit, he *wants* to be what Christ
> can make him; there is all the difference here between
> the strain of anxiety and the strain of adventure." It
> must be a major part of training to help men and women
> to see themselves as they really are and to develop a will-
> ingness to face facts, both with regard to themselves and
> the world in which they live.[8]

This basic attitude of honesty relieves a woman entirely
from all the frustrations of pretense, of preserving a front. It
keeps her humble. It helps her accept what God says to her
about herself. It gives Him a basis on which He can work in
her life as He could not otherwise.

Mr. Sargent has written also:

> But we are what we are, and we take ourselves with
> us wherever we go. Indeed in seeking to become saints,

---

[8]Douglas N. Sargent, *The Making of a Missionary* (London: Hodder
and Stoughton, 1960), p. 129.

the first thing we have to do is accept ourselves, to be natural. We shall always gain inspiration from the lives of those who live really near to our Lord, and we must learn to follow them in this while refusing to model ourselves by deliberate imitation on some saintly pattern. There must be no conscious striving after effect. Saints cannot be artificial. It is one of the deep paradoxes of the Christian life, however, that such acceptance of self must go hand in hand with a genuine despair of self. It is this despair which leads to that utter and complete dependence on God Himself which enables Him to mould us, by His Holy Spirit, into the kinds of saints which He would have us to be.

Being thus natural and "confident in self despair"—to quote Charles Wesley—a saint is humbly content . . .[9]

Truth should perhaps be second in order. God desires it to be woven into her very fiber. "Behold, thou desirest truth in the inward part," says the Psalmist who had tried to hide his sin. Given the honesty referred to above, God can work truth. Scripture states repeatedly that "lying lips are an abomination" to Him. The enemy of our souls was characterized by the Lord Jesus as the "father of lies." The heathen religions are characterized by lies, and their adherents, among whom a missionary mother works, are enslaved to lying. Warneck writes at length about this in his evaluation of animistic religions:

> It is not mere error into which the poor Animist has fallen; a positive lying power has mastered the ignorant. . . . What a fearful power of falsehood is here. . . . Deceived and defrauded in their religion the heathen are themselves given over to lying. They seem to have lost the sense for truth and honesty. . . . Lying is to them synonymous with cleverness. . . . But heathenism . . . cannot of itself overcome this power of falsehood. God

---

[9]*Ibid.*, p. 146.

alone can give back to people thus misled the truth which
they have lost.[10]

The missionary mother dares not permit anything short of
absolute truth to control her words and actions. Without it
there is no integrity.

But truth without *love* can be a fearful thing. The heart is
subject to so much selfishness, self-righteousness, pride. Until
the love of God is shed abroad in an overwhelming, purifying
flood harsh, critical, ugly thoughts and deeds will proceed
from the life. "Speaking the truth in love" is so necessary for
the missionary mother. "Unfeigned love" is so essential. Oh,
that I Corinthians 13 might be indelibly burned into every
woman's life! Only the love of God can control an unbridled
tongue. It is this love that will establish "the law of kindness
. . . in her tongue," and only God can do it.

Out of love grow the twin virtues of *patience* and *courtesy*.
Perhaps they are simply manifestations of love, but they are
areas in which, as we shall see later, the missionary mother
must particularly seek the Lord's lasting work. Her every relationship will demand them, and if they are only artificial,
her true feelings will be discovered unexpectedly, at great
detriment to the Name she seeks to honor.

Self-control, the crowning work of the Spirit in the life,
gives the key to the rest of the qualities to be mentioned. It
is as impossible of attainment as the others, except as she
walks in the Spirit, and it is as essential. Self-control is the
rule of the Holy Spirit over every avenue of life. Rather than
speak of it at length we shall point out some of the specific
areas in which it will be manifested, for without it, the Lord
does not give these other qualities.

Purity or holiness would perhaps seem a strange thing to
mention, but the missionary mother, like every other Christian, must be conscious of her constant need to be alert to
temptations to impurity in her thought life and walk. The

---

[10]Johannes Warneck (trans. Neil Buchanan), *The Living Christ and
Dying Heathenism* (Grand Rapids: Baker Book House, 1954), pp. 90-96.

enemy is quick to enter any doors left ajar through careless-ness here.

Perseverance, or faithfulness, is the quality (akin to stub-bornness) which forces a missionary on in the face of discour-agement or even defeat. It has its roots in obedience and its nourishment is faith in the living God. The missionary mother endures because she sees the Invisible.

Diligence, or industry, enables the missionary mother to accomplish far more than she could accomplish without this quality. While it is a natural quality, it must be Spirit-prompted, or her diligent service will be in her own strength and may represent wasted energy. On the other hand, Spirit-directed diligence is definitely one of the ways in which her example will influence others for good and may open up new opportunities for service. Diligence includes wisdom and skill in use of one's time, and faithfulness in oversight of the work under one's hand. A diligent person must be on her guard lest she become intolerant with those who are not as energetic and efficient as she is.

Emotional stability should be the normal experience of a Christian. "God has not given us the spirit of fear; but of power, and love, and of a sound mind" (II Tim. 1:6). The basis for all this is faith in God as the all-sufficient and un-failing One. The Christian woman who stays her heart upon God will not be afraid of evil tidings nor afflicted by resent-ment or suspicion in her relationships with others. Such feel-ings, if allowed, would affect her behavior, but a Christian woman does not need to let her moods or feelings control her.

> In dealing with souls the sagacious counsellor will al-ways draw a clear line of discrimination between what is impulsive and involuntary, and what is deliberate and voluntary. Only the latter belongs to the deeper spiritual life . . . Only by clearly understanding such distinctions can we appreciate the Divine tenderness in dealing with temperamental moods and manifestations. The Word of God constantly emphasizes not what we call *feeling* but

will. The highest virtue belongs to this plane, not of
emotion but of choice. Our feelings often sway us against
our will, and in many cases we are not responsible for
their capricious changes. But for the deliberate executive
acts of the will, which is the marshal of our being, we are
accountable; and here is the root of character, conduct,
and destiny . . . The temporary and temperamental
moods, so largely beyond our control, need not dislodge
us from our habitual unchanging purpose, living or
dying, to be the Lord's.[11]

Contributing to these last two qualities is *cheerfulness.* It
includes the "sense of humor" so prized on the mission field,
but is a larger trait. A person may not naturally be of a cheerful temperament, but it is definitely worth prayerful cultivation, especially on the mission field and in a missionary home.
In the book of Proverbs we read: "A cheerful heart is a good
medicine" (17:22). We also read, "He that is of a cheerful
heart hath a continual feast" (15:15) and "a glad heart
maketh a cheerful countenance"(15:13). But there is nothing
artificial about any of this.

Cheerfulness lives with *contentment*, a quality much to be
desired, for the Lord says that "godliness with contentment
is great gain" (I Tim. 6:6). True riches! Contentment's companion grace is *gratefulness,* or thankfulnesss, and is one of
the sure ways given in the Word by which the Christian can
glorify God. "Whoso offereth praise glorifieth me" (Ps. 50:23,
AV), says the Psalmist, and the author of Hebrews adds,
"Through him then let us offer up a sacrifice of praise to God
continually, that is, the fruit of lips which make confession to
his name" (Heb. 13:15).

One aspect of Christian living, without which this chapter
would not be complete, is the relationship between thriving,
abundant Christian life and emotional and physical health.
It is a known fact that spiritual disobedience is bound to influence health in these other areas, even as physical illness has

---

[11]Pierson, *op. cit.,* pp. 20-21.

its effect upon the emotions. So the missionary mother will need to recognize resentment, unforgiveness, pride, worry, self-seeking, jealousy, doubt, as harmful emotions from which she will seek cleansing and deliverance.

> The bitterness and resentment of the unforgiving spirit, progressing sometimes even into anger, makes for emotional tension build-up . . . When unrelieved, the condition may proceed into peptic ulcer formation.
>
> . . . In this connection it is to be pointed out that it should never be a concern to the individual involved as to whether the person or party who is apparently guilty of the wrong shows a true attitude of repentance. The principal wrong which is being done is that which one does to himself in harboring bitterness, and this causes far greater injury in most cases than can be inflicted upon him by another person. . . .
>
> As Christians, no matter who we may be, it is incumbent upon us to face these realities. . . . Forgiveness, as the central element in the Gospel, is basic. . . . There must be an attitude of finality in the transactions that take place. Merely suppressing resentments and bitterness, while hoping for a better day that never comes, is not God's method of dealing with these matters. . . . He demands, . . . a forgetting forgiveness. . . . To insist upon our rights is to insist upon something we do not deserve, . . . Only as we have a forgiving spirit do we meet the criteria needed to be recipients of God's grace in full measure. . . .[12]

A final danger warning: The missionary mother has neither time nor reason to be preoccupied with herself, physically or otherwise. She should live unto God, and all her life should be fearlessly set in His hands.

> While the missionary remains thus sensitive to the plight of others, there is no reason why he should walk about in daily fear of contracting the diseases he sees.

[12]Paul E. Adolph, *Health Shall Spring Forth* (Chicago: Moody Press, 1956), pp. 71, 74, 76.

... Once we have learned to avoid the major sources of infection, we need not be unduly worried about the existence of germs. . . . It is well to realize that most people are subject to small ailments when they first go to live in or near the tropics. Having recognized this fact and having taken all the reasonable precautions suggested to us, we should avoid over-preoccupation with matters of health. It does us no good to go about expecting to be ill.[13]

A. T. Pierson summed it up thus:

...There may be excessive self-care—too much thinking of one's self, morbidly watching every symptom and new sensation with apprehension of present or final consequences. Perfect love casts out all such tormenting fear. There must be some remedy for all these nervous conditions; otherwise we should be helpless victims of disorders which have much to do with mental and spiritual states. We have an unchangeable conviction that the lesson taught in Philippians 4 about habitual rejoicing in the Lord, prayerful abandonment of anxious thought, engrossment of heart with divine things, resolute contentment with His appointment, confidence in His all-sufficient strength and in His exhaustless supplies for all possible needs, furnish a solution to the problem of nervous ailments.[14]

A missionary mother whose four children are now adults, three of them foreign missionaries, and whose life is unusually active, rich, and fruitful, added this notation to the questionnaire she returned:

Remember that God's major work in a missionary is not primarily missionary work, but rather His sovereign dealing in the life of that missionary, His purchased possession, preparing her for eternity; causing her to grow in grace and in the knowledge of His Son, the Lord Jesus Christ; forming in her the image of His Son and

---

[13]Douglas Sargent, *op. cit.,* p. 125.
[14]A. T. Pierson, *op. cit.,* p. 116.

giving expression to His eternal desire for communion with His dear child. Only then it is that missionary labors become Spirit-motivated, Spirit-produced, and Spirit-empowered.

God has a loving design in every circumstance. Trustingly and fully collaborate with Him, and rest in Him. "From faith unto faith: as it is written, but the righteous shall live by faith" (Rom. 1:17).

CHAPTER 2

HER HUSBAND

. . . So when, in that autumn he said, "Will you join your life with mine for China?" my answer was "Yes," without a moment's hesitation. But a few days later when he said, "Will you give me your promise that *always* you will allow me to *put my Lord and His work first, even before you?*" I gave an inward gasp before replying, "Yes, I will, *always.*"[1]

W OMAN WAS CREATED, at the very first, to fill the need of man. That still remains her prime responsibility and joy. Not only so, but the God who made her has given her the possibility of meeting his need. She is "an help *meet* for him." "Ideally suited," says the Spanish. A help "corresponding to or over against him," says Gesenius' *Hebrew and Chaldee Lexicon.* The Berkeley Version of the Bible translates this expression in Genesis this way: "a suitable helper, completing him."

Even now it is true that while houses and riches are an inheritance from fathers, a prudent wife is from the Lord. The wonderful "wife chapter" in Proverbs says, "The heart of her husband trusteth in her, and he shall have no lack of gain (Prov. 31:11).

A wife is her husband's companion. She should also consider their relationship one of friendship—a friendship that grows stronger and fresher with the years. She studies his tastes and interests and learns to tell a carburetor from a crankshaft,

[1]Rosalind Goforth, *Goforth of China* (Grand Rapids: Zondervan Publishing House, 1940), p. 49.

a scalpel from a suture. This friendship will help to keep their life on the field on an even keel.

Their reciprocal love is God's provision of one of their deepest needs. It is given to her both to love and to delight her husband. She is to be a garden enclosed, a fountain sealed (Song of Solomon 4:12), just for him. The joy of this relationship, savored constantly in the presence of the holy God who has given it, brings a very real sense of fulfillment and rest to both.

The wife must carefully preserve herself entirely for her husband. In ordinary life such carefulness is necessary, but in a foreign land where she is representing the Bride of Christ, the importance of the utmost discretion in social relationships with other men cannot be exaggerated.

The missionary and his wife are coworkers, and more so perhaps than most pastors and their wives in the homeland. Douglas Sargent wrote,

> On the mission field there is normally a more vital community of interest, the wife being deeply concerned with the preaching of the Gospel, the husband better placed to play his full part within the narrower limits of family life . . .[2]

They are both actively engaged in the evangelization of non-Christians and the building up of believers in the area where they work. The various facets of their individual responsibilities are closely interrelated. If she be a faithful woman, not given to spreading news, she will serve as a repository of problems, opinions, counsel, and help.

There is need of objectivity in this interchange. A husband and wife can find great blessing in jointly thinking through problems or challenges, evaluating opinions or reactions, recognizing failures or strengths, and looking to their Lord to show His way out.

The prayer fellowship between a missionary husband and

[2]Douglas Sargent, *The Making of a Missionary* (London: Hodder & Stoughton, 1960), pp. 119-20.

wife is one of the greatest assets to their ministry—if indeed it can be called just an "asset" and not a ministry in itself. The sharing of needs for prayer can be full and unrestrained. The blessings of united prayer are at their immediate command. And the missionary couple who avail themselves of this avenue of service with God enjoy the added richness of fellowship in the Gospel and untold blessing in their work.

Strangely enough, the Scriptures indicate a close interrelation between a strong, effectual prayer ministry and marital harmony. "Defraud ye not one the other except it be by consent for a season, that ye may give yourselves unto prayer, and may be together again . . ." (I Cor. 7:5) can apply to the experience of a couple in Christian work, burdened with their own spiritual need or with that of those about them.

In I Peter 3:7 Peter exhorts husbands, "Dwell with your wives according to knowledge, giving honor unto the woman, as unto the weaker vessel, as being joint-heirs of the grace of life; to the end that your prayers be not hindered."

If their prayers before God are hindered by disharmony, by lack of mutual subjection, by a failure to discipline themselves, how much more is the testimony of husband and wife nullified before others by the quick retort, the flare of rebellion, the thoughtless act!

When a couple become conscious of these or other situations, they are wise to face them quickly before the Lord because their behavior is to be *seemly* among the Gentiles (I Peter 2:12).

Dr. Henry Brandt, a Christian psychologist, speaks of this as "a process of rebuke and forgive," pointing out that when the Lord Jesus said, "Rebuke him," He did not mean "a good tongue lashing." In one of his case histories, Dr. Brandt speaks of bickering and quarreling as "spiritual termites that were destroying their whole being."[3] To a missionary from a tropical country, the figure of termites is a strong one.

[3]Henry Brandt, *Happy Family Life* (Lincoln, Nebraska: Back to the Bible Broadcast, 1963), pp. 17, 54.

The married woman's ministry is primarily to her husband, as Paul pointed out (I Cor. 7:34). If she considers the text in the light of all Bible teaching on the subject, she finds that this is precisely what the Lord expects. By serving her husband, she is fulfilling God's plan for her; to neglect him is to disobey God's will.

Scripture teaching is equally clear as to her position of subjection to her husband. This, in addition to furnishing a picture of Christ and the Church before the world, provides a working basis for smooth family living. If she finds it hard to bend to her husband's wishes, she will be helped if she can accept this as the Lord's way of making her truly beautiful, working in her a meek and quiet spirit, which is called an *ornament* which in the sight of God is of great price, or very precious.

Sometimes a woman is rebellious at being overruled by her husband in some decision or hampered in the way she wishes to go. If she and her husband can face their conflicts before the Lord, they are sure to find both a solution, and a release from pent-up strain and bitterness. Such conflicts are an un-necessary strain, and should be eliminated immediately, though their complete eradication may take time and long patience.

Some missionary husbands are unreasonable, selfish, and thoughtless. The wife still has protection. Her husband is at least a Christian, and as she prays for him and for herself, the God who answers prayer will work in them both. He can also enable her to accept without bitterness, in growing love, what formerly frustrated and angered her.

Every married couple must learn to talk over problems, expressing themselves fully and freely. Surely in I Corinthians 13, in Ephesians 5, in I Peter 3, I John 4, they will find com-mon ground on which to meet. As at other times, honesty and a very tender frankness are a prerequisite for a mutual understanding of their problems. For this reason they will want to ask the Lord to enable them to speak the truth in love.

The only successful way to handle the obstacles in the road to a happy married life in the parsonage is to learn the technique of praying things through and talking things out. To harbor misunderstanding or to allow resentment to develop is a sure beginning of a breach. But to talk out the problem calmly, centering the discussion on the issue, rather than on the person, is an expression of adult emotional maturity. . . .

Real happiness in the parsonage does not come by ideal circumstances; it comes when two people, eager in God's service, have learned enough about each other to love in spite of shortcomings, in spite of unpleasant surroundings, in spite of long hard days at work.[4]

Never should a wife criticize her husband to nationals, fellow missionaries, children, or others. The antidote to a critical spirit is the development of the habit of thinking appreciatively about the good qualities of a person. If she tells her husband about his good qualities or gives him an honest compliment occasionally, he will find her words to be a source of strength and encouragement.

Much of her ministry to her husband will be in the realm of the ordinary and the routine. Still, there are married women who after twenty, thirty, or more years of caring for their husband's needs still find keen delight in every service they can render them. This is an attitude of mind which can be fostered, and can add luster to a woman's daily living. She is doing it for him as unto the Lord.

A missionary wife will help her husband by making their home as attractive as possible. Plants, a few yards of print or color, artistic use of anything from books to rocks, careful planning of furniture placing for greatest convenience and attractiveness, skillful use of paint if practicable, can make the lowliest hut spell "home" to a missionary.

---

[4]Lora Lee Parrott, *How to be a Preacher's Wife and Like It.* (Grand Rapids: Zondervan Publishing House, 1956), p. 22.

She ought to keep that home clean and in order. An aged mission executive observed in an interview, "A missionary home kept like a pigsty is a woeful thing . . . and I have seen such."

She will need to discipline herself to bother him as little as possible with the details of running the household so as to leave him free for his ministry.

She should serve nutritious meals as attractively as possible, always bearing in mind that his health, and that of her family, are to a great degree in her hands.

She should strive to keep his clothes in good repair—and this is quite a feat for some missionary wardrobes, especially as a term on the field nears its end.

She can plan to relieve him of the greater part of the burden of letter-writing, saving him hours upon hours of time. Most missionary wives assume this responsibility.

She should share actively in many ways in the ministry to which they have given themselves, assisting him in public or in private, but keeping always in the background. She will take over, especially, in the follow-up of women converts and children.

She should protect him, if possible, from interruption in times when he desires to be alone for study or for prayer.

A faithful missionary wife will share in her husband's prayer burdens, and where she sees either lacks or problems in his ministry, she will pray faithfully for him. She will seek, with the Lord's help, to make any suggestions lovingly and constructively.

A wise missionary wife will refrain from pushing her husband into places of prominence when he does not feel the Lord is leading him into them. She will rather encourage him to fulfill to the best of his ability the type of ministry to which he feels called.

She will ask the Lord to guard her heart from any taint of jealousy, and to teach her rather the ways of trust, helpfulness, and full delight in her dear one. She will recognize his worth, and show it in a hundred quiet ways.

She will make every effort to be attractive for him, even out in the jungle or just "at home." Neatness and cleanliness and a happy spirit are irresistible companions.

She will cultivate the qualities of sympathy, perception, and courage which will enable her to strengthen him when he is in need, whatever the cause. She has every reason to do this. The word of God to a Christian is to "be strong, and of a good courage," and the message is reiterated all through Scripture. These qualities come, however, as the work of God when a woman is in daily contact with Him. As she hears God speaking to her when she reads His Word and prays, she will be able to encourage her husband because she has been encouraged. How wonderful if she can say, "The Lord Jehovah hath given me the tongue of them that are taught, that I may strengthen with words him that is weary: he wakeneth, morning by morning, he wakeneth mine ear to hear as they that are taught" (Isaiah 50:4).

She will learn to weigh the present in the balance with eternity, and in this fashion will counsel with her husband.

While it is true that all missionary wives do not do all these things (there are a few husbands, for example, who take care of the family correspondence and enjoy it), the fact still remains that most of them do all these things and more, and still find occasion to serve the Lord in the different avenues He indicates.

One missionary wife summed up her service to her husband in this beautiful way:

> I help my husband by making my ministry and home duties fit in with his so that his ministry is not often restricted by home duties, and by sharing with him the spiritual burden of the work even when I am not taking an active part in it.

The surprising, humbling fact is this, that in the end the

faithful, loving, helpful, wise missionary wife finds she has been a living illustration to the people among whom they minister, an illustration of what God would have the Christian wife to be. What has seemed to her a simple, hidden ministry will be crowned with unexpected fruit, unconsciously borne.

There is a paradox in the life of the missionary wife. While her husband means more to her than her life, and her closeness to him is a thing she could never put into the poverty of words, she is capable of complete spiritual independence apart from him. The spiritual fellowship in the Lord of a missionary husband and wife is one of the inexpressibly precious things of life. Laboring together for the Lord whom both love supremely is a wonderful experience—a gift of God. And, as with all His other gifts, the greatest joy comes as she finds the Giver greater than the gift.

The missionary wife, then, can willingly, even gladly, be separated over and over from her husband, even if she never gets over the heartache of it. She can encourage him to obey freely whatever plans the Lord has for him. She herself will be dependent upon the Lord alone for all physical, emotional, and spiritual good, all satisfaction and joy; for in a real way she will come to understand the words, "Thy Maker is thine husband" (Isa. 54:5).

The story of missions is full of such wives—not necessarily heroic women but just women who loved their husbands and the Lord. One such received this tribute from her husband, William Carey of India:

> I am now called in Divine Providence to be a mourner again, having lately experienced the greatest domestic loss that a man can sustain. My dear wife was removed from me by death on Wednesday morning, May 30th, about twenty minutes after midnight. . . . She was eminently pious, and lived very near to God. The Bible was her daily delight, and next to God she lived only for me.

Her solicitude for my happiness was incessant, and so certainly could she at all times interpret my looks, that any attempt to conceal anxiety or distress of mind would have been in vain. Nothing, however, but tenderness for each other's feelings could induce either of us for a minute to attempt a concealment of anything. It was her constant habit to compare every verse she read in the various German, French, Italian, and English versions, and never to pass by a difficulty until it was cleared up. In this respect she was of eminent use to me in the translation of the Word of God. She was full of compassion for the poor and needy, . . . She entered most heartily into all the concerns of the mission, and into the support of schools, particularly those for female native children, . . . So many merciful circumstances attend this very heavy affliction as still yield me support beyond anything I ever felt in other trials. (1) I have no domestic strife to reflect on, and add bitterness to affliction. (2) She was ready to depart. She had long lived on the borders of the heavenly land, and I think lately became more and more heavenly in her thoughts and conversation."[5]

---

[5]John B. Myers, *William Carey* (London: S. W. Partridge & Co., Ltd., 1887), pp. 99-100.

CHAPTER 3

HER CHILDREN

T HE CHILDREN OF MISSIONARIES were characterized by Edward Judson as "the involuntary inheritors of their parents' sufferings and reward" in the dedication of his *Life of Adoniram Judson*. Since Edward Judson was "one of them," he spoke from experience.

A POTENTIAL ASSET

Missionary children can also be characterized as potential assets on the field. I use the term "potential" because those little lives hold such great possibilities for good or evil, and their influence on the Lord's work can be so far-reaching. Over and over again mothers have written about this influence. For instance:

> The presence of a baby son has been a blessing in a Muslim land.
> The Japanese love children. My husband says, "When I got married, I felt myself heightened in the estimation of the Japanese; and when our first child was born, I went up another notch." Likewise the same could be said when our first boy arrived. Children do away with ceremony, break down barriers, become a natural invitation into the home. I could go on . . .
> The children do make an entrance into many homes and hearts. Their facility in the language and unaffected friendliness do much. Nearly everyone loves children.
> We wouldn't be able to do it differently but we do wish that the Lord had given us children. It is wonderful to have a home that we can invite nationals into. We

have felt that children would have given more of an
openness with our Indian people, however.

It may be stated categorically that the presence of a loving, friendly, well-behaved missionary child is one of the greatest possible blessings in missionary work. Conversely, a missionary child who is not born again, or who has not continued to grow in grace, is a veritable weapon in the hand of
the Enemy for the undermining of a Christian work. Every
one of the lovely babes given to missionary parents is a potential Hophni or Phinehas or a Samuel.

Even Dr. William Carey, the great missionary to India, had
both kinds of sons. In London, during the annual meeting of
the Baptist Missionary Society, a speaker referred to Dr.
Carey as having two of his sons, Felix and William, devoted
to the mission.

"But," said he, "there is a third who gives him pain;
he is not yet turned to the Lord." Then, making a solemn
pause, during which tears flowed abundantly from his
eyes, he exclaimed in a voice which seemed to exhaust a
whole soul of feeling: "Brethren, let us send up a united,
universal, and fervent prayer to God in solemn silence
for the conversion of Jabez Carey."As though the Holy
Ghost had suddenly fallen upon the assembly, the whole
congregation, of at least two thousand persons, betook
themselves to silent intercession. Think we that the Lord
spake in vain when He said, "Pray ye the Lord of the
harvest"? One of the first letters afterwards received bore
the news of the conversion of this son, who up to this
time "had greatly pained his father by his apparent dislike of religion"; and the time of his awakening was
found to accord almost exactly with the hour of this
memorable intercession. Immediately on his conversion
he presented himself for missionary service at Am-
boyna, . . . "I trust," said the good father, "that this will
be a matter of everlasting praise. Oh, praise the Lord
with me, and let us exalt His name together! To me the
Lord has been very gracious. I trust all my children love

the Lord; and three out of four are actually engaged in
the important work of preaching the gospel among the
heathen, two of them in new countries."[1]

This matter of the behavior of the children of Christian
workers is so important that Paul said that the "bishop" must
be "one that ruleth well his own house, having his children
in subjection with all gravity" (I Tim. 3:4-5); also, "Let deacons be husbands of one wife, ruling their children and their
own houses well" (I Tim. 3:12).

> The man who forges ahead to accomplish things has
> to find the time somewhere, and the easiest place is to
> steal it from the family. Unless he plans his time so that
> the family gets something near to normal home life, the
> missionary may find his greatest mission field is his own
> home. It is possible to gain a church, and lose a home,
> for which he is also responsible to God. . . .
>
> On the other hand, the family has to understand that
> the missionary is called to spend much time at the work
> away from home. Sharing in his work by understanding
> will be a great help. If the family can feel the cooperative
> basis of their witness, they will be happier, and be a
> better testimony to the nationals.[2]

The comments of different missionary children reflected
both a sense of having missed much companionship with their
fathers and an appreciation of the time their fathers did spend
with them. For instance, the son of a missionary who necessarily traveled very much wrote:

> The relationship between missionary children and
> their parents is a very vital one. While the missionary is
> a "full-time" minister of the Gospel, he or she has
> the same responsibility to the Lord in raising children as

---

[1]A. J. Gordon, *The Holy Spirit in Missions* (London: Hodder and
Stoughton, 1896), pp. 88-89.

[2]Ruth N. Campbell, "Rearing and Educating Missionary Children in a
Foreign Environment" (unpublished Master's thesis, Fuller Theological
Seminary, 1958), p. 43.

does any other Christian parent. A missionary father is still a father; a missionary mother is still a mother. As the children grow up, they should not have reason to regard their parents as "Uncle Daddy" and "Aunt Mommy."

Often the male parent is the more involved in the work that is associated with the foreign missionary— overseeing the local church, visiting or traveling to the nearby villages. In spite of all his duties, he still needs to spend a definite time with his wife and children. While there is involved a sacrifice of time with his family, I don't believe the Lord wants the unity and spiritual growth of the family members to suffer as a result of the father's being busy or away from them much of the time.

A PRIMARY RESPONSIBILITY

Earlier in this study the peculiar responsibility of the mother in child-rearing was noted. Speaking of the mother's responsibility on the mission field, it has been well written:

> If her absence from home means a loss of the testimony of a dynamic Christian family, in the long run she has missed the best means of witness among a people that need the example of Christian lives to follow. . . . To the same extent they will be a hindrance to the gospel their parents hope to present, if the children's lives do not measure up in any way to what the parents teach.[3]

A second conclusion may be reached, then, that it is a primary responsibility, especially for missionary parents, that their children be carefully, wisely reared, and specially nurtured in the things of the Lord.

The questionnaires indicated that mothers are very conscious of this fact. One mother said, "I cannot neglect my children and expect them to follow the Lord," while another wrote:

> Our children will be the witnesses to the coming gen-

---

[3]*Ibid.*

eration. If we succeed in winning the heathen, and lose our own children, we have failed to fulfill God's plan for us. I believe that God will lead us and enable us to keep the balance we need in this important matter.

The rearing of children is so important to the missionary because it is a very personal responsibility, specifically entrusted to those parents into whose hands the Lord put the baby. No amount of busy-ness here and there (cf. I Kings 20:39-40) will excuse a woman before God for carelessness about this specific trust put upon her.

The "ruling of the house" is the scriptural responsibility of the father—and the missionary child is fortunate whose life has been enriched by close fellowship with his father. A missionary's son wrote:

> When Bill and I were about nine and eleven, respectively, Dad read to us a book, a baseball story called *The Young Pitcher*. It was one of those books that leaves the reader with a desire to keep reading. How we enjoyed Dad's reading *The Young Pitcher* to us! While I am strong on the father's spending time with his children, the fact is that it is the father who usually spends less time with his children than his wife.

A man who is careful to take time for family life will build stability in his children and will also have rounded out the picture of family living that is such a powerful witness for the Gospel in a heathen land.

> . . . Just as it is sometimes too lightly assumed that, because two Christians marry, the result is a Christian family. . . . it is true that the first essential on the upbringing of children is a family where father and mother obviously love one another—love for the children being the second essential—so also, when the wider influence of the family is concerned, it is necessary that love should be seen to be of the very essence of its fabric. . . . By Bible study and prayer, by frank and open discussion,

they must be drawn ever closer together as they face the ever-changing pattern of life, and so be able as a family to present a united witness of love to those who come within the orbit of the family.[4]

But in the nature of the case, by far the greater part of the children's training will come from the hands of their mother, whose place it is to "guide the house." Until she realizes that this has scriptural sanction, she will probably find it to be the most perplexing problem facing her. Here is the very heart of the missionary mother. *How* can she be fully a missionary, and fully a mother?

The problem arises from the premise that missionary work and motherhood are mutually exclusive callings. This in turn comes from the unconscious feeling that a woman's children are her own, and that when she cares for them she is spending time on her own interests. It is a warped point of view, as one woman finally realized:

> A weary missionary eased her child's emaciated body onto the toilet and then, steadying the child with one arm, leaned against the wall. She felt numb at heart, exhausted; and the fact that the child had been pronounced beyond the physician's skill seemed temporarily to fade in importance before the cry of her blinded heart: "Oh, if it were just some little orphan, it would be for the Lord!"
>
> The story is true; and in that moment the woman's whole concept of missionary life was corrected in wave upon wave of repentance and confession as the Lord brought her to her senses. That child was no more hers than an orphan would be!

Apart from the details, this is hardly an isolated experience. Every conscientious missionary mother has faced it on one ground or another. As one mother wrote on her questionnaire: "It has been a conflict to accept the children as my first responsibility." It is especially hard for the woman who was

---

[4]Douglas N. Sargent (London: Hodder & Stoughton, 1960), p. 118.

formerly a single missionary to accept the seeming limitations of motherhood. She is so conscious of her call to missionary service and so sensible of the richness the Lord has poured upon her that she can easily determine never to allow anything to hinder her "work" for the Lord. A mother must choose; and the right choice is clear.

> Our small children are our first responsibility before the Lord. There is ample Scripture to back up this stand. A lady doctor of the China Inland Mission—OMF—who has delivered four of our children has been of great help to frustrated mothers, helping them to realize that their chief concern should be for their youngsters, especially during the tender years when, in a foreign country, their only real anchor is their mother. And for children who must leave home for school at an early age, the preschool years of teaching by their mother are all-important. Every child should have a salvation experience before going away to school—which would mean at the age of six or before.
>
> Since I feel He led me into this marriage, then I feel equally that He intended for me to work and spend half my time in mission service and the other three-fourths in the home! If I can rear these wonderful little children to love Him with all their hearts, all their minds, and all their souls, then I feel my greatest task shall be accomplished.

Missionary children grow up; and what they will become is, humanly speaking, in their mothers' hands. A young man, now in college, wrote:

> The mother is often not as involved in the missionary work as the father. Normally speaking, I think this is right. Raising a family is a full-time job, and although Mom is not the only parent, much of the responsibility of caring for and rearing the children will fall on her. Sometimes it will be necessary for Dad to be away, and in his absence Mom has a double load of duty. She will

not be able to fulfill the task if she is bound by many other obligations.

I can remember the baking days in————. Mom would give each of us a piece of dough, and while she made cinnamon rolls and bread, we would make something that was supposed to be a turtle or we would try our hand at a small cinnamon roll. My brother and I surely enjoyed these days. Mom was not so busy that she couldn't spare us a little time—and dough!

Such incidents through which Mom showed her interest and love toward us bound us closer to her, I believe. And when one knows that his mother loves him, and has seen this love, I believe he will find it easier to respond to her correction and instruction.

A child's first needs are for love and security, which the missionary parents are well equipped to provide especially if they can realize that God has set them free to do this very thing. Love is theirs in full measure, shed abroad in their hearts by the Holy Spirit, and they can learn to show it at all times and in all situations. As for security, what greater security can parents impart to their children than the security they themselves have found in the unchanging, living God?

> The things a missionary child needs most from his parents are those that any child needs: genuine love and affection, a feeling of belonging and being wanted, reasonable but firm discipline, more commendation than criticism, and much patience and prayer.[5]
>
> Of course a child who is respected as an individual will never be compared with other children in the family, or ridiculed or belittled for his ideas. . . . A child needs to feel loved for his own sake, not for what he can do or how he looks or acts.
>
> . . . the need for "verbalized approval." Honest praise for a task well done, told in the presence of the father and child so the father can praise him too, can go a long

---

[5]Wallace R. Wright—Dr. Clyde Narramore, personal letter, Nov. 6, 1963.

way toward helping a child develop into his best, and create a strong family relationship of love and appreciation. . . . Recognizing honest effort, even when the result is not always achieved, helps cover the hurt of failure and encourages one to try again.[6]

The discussion of the question of first responsibility as it came out in the questionnaires was of particular interest. Here is the primary battleground of the mother-missionary conflict. Every mother had had to face the dilemma to find what was for her a working solution. In no sense is this an unusual problem. Every working mother has had to face it, and every mother who has decided not to work. The difference is that in the missionary situation it becomes a matter of conscience rather than of financial necessity; and conscience can be a driving taskmaster. The philosophical or moral implications will be discussed in a subsequent chapter, but the studied opinion of so many mothers should yield a few guiding principles to consider at this point.

The questionnaire asked: "Do you feel that your children or your missionary work are your first responsibility before the Lord?"

Sixty-eight answered, "Children," with the added notation in many cases, "while they are young," or "till they are grown." One wrote, "This has been a frustrating problem to me," while another said, "It's hard to answer." Only one mother felt her missionary work to be her first responsibility. Her two daughters were near teen-agers, and the questionnaire revealed that the children work closely with her.

With these as background, the remaining answers become decidedly helpful to this study .

"I do not believe them to be mutually exclusive," wrote one. "I'd therefore say both."

"Neither. Each has its rightful place," wrote another.

"Both were completely dedicated to Him," said still another.

---

[6]Ruth N. Campbell, *op. cit.*, pp. 72,27.

"I believe God helped me to be effective as a mother and as I went out as a missionary."

"I have not divided my life up this way," was another woman's reaction.

The questionnaire asked further: "Do you often feel that to fully meet the one responsibility you must be less effective in the other?"

For purposes of this study, the answers were entirely satisfactory. They ranged widely from several who wrote "Yes!!!" on through "Yes, at times," and "Yes, somewhat," to "Not necessarily," or "No, but I believe it is a common occurrence," and "No; one helps the other, not hinders."

Many of the mothers expained their answers at this point. To quote several:

> Yes, I have felt that way, but I don't think it's really true. They really work together.
>
> You have less time, but on the other hand a good mother has a testimony before the national women.
>
> Yes, but it all depends what kind of standard you're using. . . . We have our children only until they are seven, and it is well known how much the early years mean in a child's development in all phases.
>
> I feel the Lord wants me to care for my children and husband. Sometimes it affects the work.
>
> Yes, that is often what one feels. But I never take any responsibility that will conflict with my responsibility to my husband or my children when they are at home.
>
> If effectiveness is based on time spent, yes, but I believe in pioneer missionary work a Christian family bears a testimony and accomplishes something that teaching by word alone can not do.

A mother whose eight children are nearly all grown summarized the relationship of motherhood to missionary responsibility thus:

> It is my belief that other missionary effort, should it

result in the actual neglect of the children's needs, will not be worth much in the long run. I like to paraphrase the Scripture, "What shall it profit a mother if she gains the heathen world and loses the soul of her own child?"

But I do not mean by this that I have not been able to have a ministry along with rearing my family. I have a good working knowledge of the language, have taught English classes, played the organ for church, for three years was in charge of our Mission Center with its language students and stream of guests, have taught music at our Bible school. At present I am teaching nine piano and organ lessons a week, and am beginning to teach a weekly English class of approximately forty young women. We are boarding a niece during the week so that she can attend our little grade school for missionary children in this area. If our two little boys begin attending kindergarten, my free time will be further broadened, and my never-satisfied mind conceives many ways in which I will occupy that time.

A second expressed it this way:

Each detracts and each adds to the other. Let me explain: I feel I'm a better mother for having stimulating interests outside the home. My responsibility, before the Lord, is to be a good part-time teacher in the Biblical Seminary, and to be a good mother the rest of the time. The two are not mutually exclusive. There are times when I put in less time than I ought to on class preparation because of home responsibilities. On the other hand, the experiences of homemaking and motherhood have prepared me to be a better teacher, friend, and counselor to the students.

One other wrote:

I believe there is a balance. The Lord should come first in our hearts, but the work at hand must be done whether it is to care for the children or to do housework. That does not mean one's heart is out of communion with the Lord. It is God's will to do what lies before us. . . .

Surely we cannot neglect our children. I think the Lord means for a missionary mother to learn the balance in serving both her family and the missionary work before her. . . . So I would not say a mother was less effective because she is giving a testimony of Christ by the home life, how to conduct the family, serve them and others, even if she cannot be out with the people as the single worker can.

Reading through the questionnaires, one becomes conscious of a strong current of feeling running through them. All these mothers had accepted their children as a God-given, personal responsibility, but nearly all seemed impelled by another ever present and equally powerful drive—the missionary responsibility—which would become more so as their children reached maturity. For this reason there were answers such as these to the aforementioned questions:

The children are first, but should not be used as an excuse to neglect missionary work.

I have tried not to go to extremes, either of leaving my children completely to the care of nationals, nor of so tying myself to the home that I have no time for other work and witness.

The children are first, but that does not exclude the other. . . . There is a God-given happy medium when one can know priorities.

My children are included in my missionary work. I do not feel a woman should cease her missionary activity because of motherhood.

The children first, but I have tried by His grace not to let them stand in the way of the Lord's work. I believe He gives wisdom in all things as they come, to know what to do at the time.

I feel my children come first but that does not make me less a missionary. I still have my obligations and must fulfill them. There often have been frustrations, but if

we find God's will for each hour of the day, there will be
no conflict.

A POWERFUL CHALLENGE

With this reminder that the mother is, indeed, still a
missionary, let us now consider some of the challenging
aspects of child-rearing on a foreign mission field.

One missionary child, now in college, wrote:

> I think my parents brought me up on the field the
> same as they would have in the States. I don't know any-
> thing else to say about it. I do consider it an advantage
> to have been an MK (Colloquial term commonly used to
> mean "Missionary Kid").

Facts being what they are, however, this sense of security
comes from proper orientation of the life. The only stable
elements in the life of a missionary child are his parents and
the Lord. The Lord will never fail him; but, at least in his
early years, it is his parents who represent the Lord to him.
This is why parents must walk so carefully before the Lord,
in love for each another and for their children, that they may
be kept unerringly in His ways.

> For the child to be secure, there must also be a secure
> relationship of deep affection between his parents. True
> mutual love results in fullness of personal and individual
> life that produces satisfaction apart from the child. On
> the other hand, parents not bound to each other by ties
> of strong affection are likely to seek in the affection of
> the child, or by domination of him, satisfaction for their
> unfulfilled desires. The child feels a sense of security in
> his parents' love for each other. When he senses that
> there is a real love relationship between them, he comes
> to love both of them, thus finding a secure support for
> the beginning of his own emotional development. The
> capacity to love is largely dependent on being loved by
> one's parents, or parent-substitutes, during infancy.[7]

[7]C. B. Eavey, *Principles of Personality Building for Christian Parents,*
(Grand Rapids: Zondervan Publishing House, 1952) p. 104.

What experience can be sweeter for a mother than to speak to the ear of her newborn babe the name of Jesus, and the wonder of a life given over completely to Him? If spiritual instruction continues through each day of the mother's (and father's) lives, as Deuteronomy 11:19 commands ("And ye shall teach them your children, talking of them, when thou sittest in thy house, and when thou walkest by the way, and when thou liest down, and when thou risest up"), as the infant becomes a toddler, and the toddler a child, the Spirit of God will be imparting spiritual truth and understanding.

One mother tells how she was presenting to her four-year-old God's claims for her life when the child's brother, not quite three, said, "I want to ask Jesus to come into my heart." Half fearful, she dared not insist he wait till he was older and understood better. They prayed together and the transaction was made. A few minutes later he said, "Mommy—" and climbed into his crib. "Mommy, Jesus is God." And that little one so early "born again," has continued to grow in grace and in the knowledge of God to young manhood.

This is a process which the Lord works in the child's heart over a period of time, and it must be recognized that the parents' steady, consistent, loving walk with God and with the child is what the Lord would first use to bring the child to Himself. From then on, as the stereo record is centered on its spindle, so the child's life is centered in Christ, and is guided and moved by the turntable of parental guidance and parental discipline. In commenting on this, a missionary daughter introduced an interesting figure of speech:

> I think the MK and every other child needs practical applications of spiritual truths to be made specific to him. In the basics we are all the same. Our different experiences and ways of life are just the strings of this practical outworking. We need our parents' help constantly, especially when we are younger, to keep our strings attached to the center reason for all—the Lord Jesus.

Missionary child-rearing differs from that of ordinary American families in two important respects: it takes place in the midst of two cultures, and it is inevitably keyed to the separation that must come sooner or later.

EARLY YEARS AT HOME

This separation is one of the more painful experiences of missionary life, but since it is inescapable, the missionary parents are wise to accept it as part of the Lord's will for them right from the start. Surely they must pray earnestly about the matter; but they can also trust, for the Lord will guide them. Having accepted the coming separation, they will begin early to train their children in making choices wisely, in forming judgments of right and wrong, in general independence. A mother will be sympathetic and helpful, but she will not tie her children to herself. She will form a "horizontal," friend-to-friend relationship with her child rather than encouraging a "vertical" or leaning, "sun-satellite" dependence. This attitude in no way rules out a child's respect for his parent, nor the parent's care for the child, but it does teach self-reliance from an early age.

The question of education of missionary children is not nearly so serious in modern times as it formerly was. There are many fine schools available to missionary children on most mission fields now, and transportation has so improved over the years that now the separation through the early grades is at most for a few months at a time.

Still, the schools are no finer than their personnel, and when the ideals and opinions or principles of these differ from those of the parents, they can cause many heartaches. Always, there is still a separation; and for the sake of all concerned, parents should bring their children to an early, matter-of-fact acceptance of the situation—even if, as one mother wrote, "it hurts." She added, "The children adjust fine, but *others* have the greatest influence on their lives."

Meanwhile, the parents have those children during the first

six or seven years of their lives at the very least. These early years are of prime importance in child training, and it is right that a mother take all the time necessary to inculcate in her children the primary virtues of obedience, truth, faithfulness, generosity, and self-control in their various manifestations. The Scriptures speak clearly concerning these things. Proverbs 22:6 says: "Train up a child in the way he should go, and even when he is old he will not depart from it."

DISCIPLINE

Correction of a small child is not difficult. It requires the full attention of the mother at that moment, and it must be given quietly, without excitement, but with authority. The parents should agree on what they feel most important (he can't learn it all at once!), and give correction as teaching along those lines. Small children will obey temporarily at first, and then for longer periods of time. In the same way that a child learns through feeling, touching, handling, the Lord has ordered that he learn to obey through physical chastisement. The hand that pulls books out of the forbidden bookcase, or that scribbles in a hymn book, should be quietly but decisively slapped, and the parent watches so as to administer the same punishment again immediately if necessary. Very likely it *will* be necessary till the child has satisfied himself that the parent is in earnest and that there is no way to sidestep that ruling.

This periodic testing of authority is typical of the growing child in a well-ordered home, and should be met by the parent with patience and firmness. The important thing is that the parents be agreed and that they consistently require obedience. It is well that they uphold each other's authority before the child, never willfully overruling each other.

Parents must learn to discern and discriminate in punishment between what is accidental and what was intentional; but when the accidental has a tendency to become habitual, a parent will have to punish simply to stimulate a child's memory and judgment. Punishment is *not* vindictive in the Christian home. The parents' aim in punishing is the child's development and establishment in right ways, for Proverbs 22:15 says: "Foolishness is bound up in the heart of a child; but the rod of correction shall drive it far from him."

There seems to come a time in the first three or four years when a child willfully sets himself to challenge his parents' authority. This is a crucial experience, and the parents need to dedicate themselves, for the time being, to bringing him through to complete obedience. Utmost patience and perseverance are required, and great discernment, and it is much better if both parents can be free to deal with the child, one giving himself to prayer while the other reasons and disciplines. It may take hours or even days, for the child is often tired, and one must deal gently, lovingly, and yet very firmly with him; but in time the Lord enables the child to bend his will to that of his parents, and the first great battle on the way to maturity has been won. This is an exhausting experience, but it is nothing to the heartbreak that comes from bringing up an undisciplined child. The book of Proverbs (23:13-14; 19:18) speaks with authority when it says:

> Withhold not correction from the child;
> For if thou beat him with the rod, he will not die.
> Thou shalt beat him with the rod,
> And shalt deliver his soul from Sheol.
> Chasten thy son, seeing there is hope;
> And set not thy heart on his destruction.

As the Lord works in a child's heart in answer to his parents' prayers, he becomes more and more willing to accept discipline. This is a work of grace, and parents dare not be satisfied without it. On the other hand, a wise love (not a selfish, lazy one) prompts them to administer any necessary discipline. Proverbs 13:24 gives a rather different evaluation to child training of this sort than some modern textbooks: "He that spareth his rod hateth his son; But he that loveth him chasteneth him betimes."

Proverbs 29:17 is a promise, and a mother can trust God

for its fulfillment. "Correct thy son, and he will give thee rest; Yea, he will give delight unto thy soul."

This type of discipline requires that the mother be fully in control of herself—*self*-disciplined. (How this drives one to her knees before the Heavenly Father!) Parents who are accustomed to using such discipline find that it can be accomplished without any rift of fellowship in the parent-child relationship, or any loss of self-respect on the part of the child. The chastening is administered for the child's profit, with no diminution of love, and the child recognizes it as such. It is also in accord with the teaching of Ephesians 6:4 "And, ye fathers, provoke not your children to wrath: but nurture them in the chastening and admonition of the Lord" and Colossians 3:21 "Fathers, provoke not your children, that they be not discouraged."

Parents in their great desire that their children be well-trained, tend to become overly demanding. This can be very discouraging to a child. Parents would do well to acquire the art of overlooking much while they and their child work one quality or degree of achievement which is within his grasp.

There is also the possibility that parents, for the sake of their own reputation or that of their child, may interfere constantly with what he does, or with the natural results of his actions. It is important that a child be allowed, occasionally, to make mistakes when they are the type that will teach him what he has not learned by simple instruction; and parents must not shield him from punishment that may come as a consequence. And it is important that he realize that he is still loved and appreciated.

Occasionally parents will find that they have punished when they should not have, or that in some way they have not acted before the child as they should have. Their reaction must be that of any other Christian or person: a complete apology. Parents have no reputation to uphold before their children but that of the Lord whom they serve; and if a parent is honest enough and humble enough to admit his mistake or make an

apology, he will impress upon his children the fact that together they are children in God's family—faulty, but beloved.
Then, when in home relationships forgiveness is expressed and
shown by parents, the children are taught valuable lessons in
forgiveness.

In such situations inevitably interested nationals will be
watching, learning, and comparing the Christian way of discipline with that of irate, non-Christian parents about them. The
faithful fulfilling of a family responsibility will become a
missionary ministry.

Obedience can be taught a child even before he can walk.
The simple word *no* with its quiet, restraining influence,
can save both him and his mother many a tear and heartache.

Truth is something else again. Like obedience, it is a quality
for which the parents must be working constantly, but which
in the end is taught of God as He reaches the heart of the
child. The trouble is that truth is something utterly foreign
to the children with whom he plays and the culture in which
he is partly growing up. Many virtues can be found among
heathen peoples, but hardly anywhere among them will you
find a love of truth. Lying to them is synonymous with clever-
ness. And God *hates* lies (Prov. 6:16-17).

This is a spiritual battle as the parents lay hold upon God
for the freeing of their children from every taint of deceit.
Parents need to be led definitely of the Spirit that they may
detect lies or deceit when they exist. Only God can give
wisdom for this. Parents must beware of prolonged distrust
and suspicion, which can ruin a parent-child relationship.

Most children of active parents, when tiny, are not lazy.
A mother does well to encourage every impulse to industry,
even if it inconveniences her slightly at the time. What one
knows how to do well, he is much more likely to enjoy doing;
and in this a mother is helping a child lay foundations for
faithfully fulfilling home responsibilities as he grows up.
Parents should consciously help children gain various skills,

for the missionary child is left to his own resources at a rather early age.

Concerning all this a missionary daughter, now taking pre-medical training in a university, wrote a summary:

> Discipline—parent must retain loving respect from children. To do this she must strive for consistency in discipline (both in herself and with her partner), for the ability to admit she is wrong sometimes and to apologize when she is, to give the children some say in certain matters that may involve discipline. The parent must primarily teach the child self-discipline—this by giving enough responsibility. The children must all share in the family work. . . .
>
> Other areas—children must *feel trusted*, and then they will feel secure. Love must be *demonstrated*, not merely had. Children should gradually be given a say in decisions; some things about the parents' work should be shared with the children. The big idea is to be a *team* for the work of God.

At this early age a child begins to learn generosity, sharing, thoughtfulness of others. Love, to a child, is a temporary feeling as a rule, dependent upon the treatment he has received from one or another person. True love is worked in his heart, as in the hearts of his parents, only by the Spirit of God. He does this in answer to prayer.

Last of all, these years must teach him the beginnings of self-control. The learning of simple obedience is one phase of this, but more must be included. He learns not to whine. He learns to eat what is set before him, whether he likes it or not. "Don't say 'I don't like,' " a seven-year-old reminded his little sister recently. "You'll be given seconds if you do." Children so trained are much easier to care for during sickness, much less embarrassing to travel with, and much more likely to eat sensibly when they grow up.

A young child learns not to cry beyond a certain point when hurt. He learns to be quiet during family prayers. He learns to control his temper. (A temper tantrum dealt with in summary, decisive, unexcited fashion is not quickly repeated, and saves both mother and child an enormous expenditure of emotional energy.) But again, the parents must rely on the Lord to work in answer to their prayers, causing this "lamb" to walk "in the paths of righteousness for his name's sake."

These early years are important for the cultivation of *ideals,* for this is the time when parents can put their stamp on their children. Perhaps the first of these—purity—could have been listed rather under "primary virtues." Certainly in later life it is closely allied to self-control. But under the tutelage of the Spirit, the ideal is early presented to the child's mind. This is so important on the mission field where, in many cases, illegitimacy and sin are the rule rather than the exception. The tiny three-year-old missionary's son who said, "Mother, . . . you know that holy thing we boys have . . .?" sent his mother before the Lord in mixed gratitude and pleading that both his body and his mind be kept always pure in the sight of a holy God.

Cleanliness and neatness begin to form a part of a child's ideals in these preschool years. Actually, the practice of cleanliness is often more easily learned at this age than later. As he gets older and impatient with all that interferes with "important" activities, he tends to dislike taking time to be neat and clean, but the roots are there, and will continue to grow if the mother is a faithful housekeeper and "taskmaster."

Other ideals parents will want to cultivate are those of courtesy and respect, love, appreciation of others, courage, and fair play. It is important to teach the child to recognize differences and to accept the fact that life treats different ones differently, and that the Lord planned it thus. A small child is capable of comprehending this, but it must be taught repeatedly. The missionary child should learn early that the world does *not* owe him a living, even if his parents *are* supported by the offerings of God's people. As he grows older, he must learn to work diligently and faithfully. His work experiences will help to teach him the value of money. He will also need to learn to use money wisely.

In the early years the appreciation of beauty can be deeply etched into a life—beauty of art, of music, of literature, of nature. The home of missionaries should have at least one or two truly fine things in it, for then a child can learn early to value and care properly for lovely things. And living with lovely things should help him to feel at home wherever the Lord takes him later.

For their children's sake, parents should examine their own tastes. Good taste can be cultivated by careful observation and comparison and by reading. Pictures should be pleasing in composition and carefully chosen, for a child lives in pictures. Books should be stimulating, but wholesome and helpful.

It is important for children to learn to enjoy good literature. Parents should take time to read to their children when they are small. A missionary's son wrote: "I think that reading to the children would be a wonderful way for a missionary mother to contribute to the oneness of the family," and a mother wrote:

> Through the years I have always enjoyed the bedtime stories with my children, especially those of preschool age. With the different ones as they grew, I have read through the Bible several times, sometimes from Hurlbut's story of the Bible and sometimes right from the Bible, simplifying the stories as I went along. Also we have been through *Pilgrim's Progress* many times. This took my evenings for many years, but I am glad now that I did it, for they are past that state—things are never quite the same when they can read their own stories after they have been to school.

Books should be carefully chosen, for much time can be wasted on what is utterly worthless. Children's classics are readily available in bookstores in the States, and there are book clubs for children which send quite good selections at a very reasonable cost. Many excellent Christian books for children have been published which are available at any Christion bookstore.

One missionary family has children who often lighten their supper dishes chore by having one of them read (anything from *As You Like It* or *Macbeth* to *Penrod,* "Hiawatha," or *Pilgrim's Progress*) to the rest while they work. Not only does the reading make the task less onerous; it also gives the family delightful, shared experiences which will be a common memory long after they are separated.

Some missionaries have never had the opportunity to learn to appreciate good music. Surely they want their children to have the opportunity they themselves missed. Fortunately, children naturally love good music, especially when they begin to hear it early; and in these days of hi-fi and battery-powered tape recorders, there is no reason why they should not hear it, even on the mission field. Even adults can easily acquire the taste for good music, if they don't already have it, for music does not need to be understood to be enjoyed. It only needs to be listened to repeatedly. Missionaries with children should be careful to include in their outfits provision for good music.

The following list of compositions includes titles contributed at random by children of missionaries and is guaranteed to please a family, even one unaccustomed to classical music.

Organ Preludes and Fugues	Bach
Symphonies 5, 6, 7	Beethoven
Hungarian Dances	Brahms
Introduction to the Orchestra	Britten
Preludes, Polonaises	Chopin
Peer Gynt Suites 1 and 2	Grieg
Piano Concerto in A Minor	Grieg
Death Valley Suite	Grofé

Grand Canyon Suite .... Grofé
The Messiah (oratorio) .... Handel
Hungarian Rhapsodies .... Liszt
Elijah (oratorio) .... Mendelssohn
Italian Symphony .... Mendelssohn
Violin Concerto in E Minor .... Mendelssohn
Peter and the Wolf .... Prokofiev
Carnival of the Animals .... Saint Saëns
Italian Concerto .... Saint Saëns
Nutcracker Suites, 1 and 2 .... Tschaikowsky
Overture of 1812 .... Tschaikowsky
Piano Concerto in B Flat Minor ...... Tschaikowsky

The list is only suggestive. It is intended to pique the interest of those who don't know where to begin. But music such as this will tend to educate the tastes of children so that they will enjoy all kinds of good music and turn away from the empty, sometimes frantic, music of the world. Because of the development of appreciation of good music, they will have discernment in judging the music of Gospel choruses and hymns. Good hymns will be more appreciated because of it.

It is good to let the children run the record player if possible. Even small children can become adept at handling records, and a few scratches are a small cost for the benefits derived.

Finally, while she has her child with her a missionary mother would teach recognition of beauty wherever it exists. Children who have been taught to find beauty everywhere will always be rich. It is not hard to make a child keenly sensitive to the delicate loveliness of a veined pebble, or raindrops strung together in the sun on a clothesline, or the marvelous construction of a beetle's leg. This appreciation, once inculcated, may take odd turns. For instance, a three-year-old brought his missionary mother a fat, green caterpillar. "Look, Mother. See the sweet worm?" And after a few minutes, "Here, Mother, here's your half of the sweet worm." Not too many months later, however, on a raw, bitter day in California, his

mother stood watching huge combers rolling in from the
Pacific to hurl themselves furiously onto the rocky beach.
A small hand slipped into hers, and after several minutes
silence an awed childish voice said, "It's a little bit . . . mag-
nificent! Isn't it, Mother?" Recognition of beauty will lead
a child to worship.

SPIRITUAL NURTURE

It has been mentioned that the Spirit of God can give
children understanding of spiritual truth at an early age.
Perhaps one of the most effective means of teaching spiritual
truth is the family devotional hour. Two missionary children
commented on the importance of this time.

> Devotions as a family are a daily must. This should
> be at a definite time and place and distinctive to the
> family in form. What it includes is not as important as its
> being a time looked forward to. Everyone should partici-
> pate in some way. The parents should not get so busy
> that family devotions are neglected. Perhaps the parents
> are *too* busy when this time is laid aside. Family worship
> and Bible study afford an excellent opportunity for in-
> struction in the doctrines of the Bible and, most of all,
> for introducing the children to the Lord and Saviour.
> (MK's need Jesus just as much as the Xingu Indians
> do.)

The program followed by most missionary families, as it
was outlined in the questionnaire responses, was to have songs
or hymns, Bible reading or the reading of a passage from a
devotional book, or Scripture memorization, discusssion and
prayer. One family makes it a habit to sing straight through
different hymnbooks so as to learn the hymns in English.
Several follow definite prayer training and prayer guidance
programs. One family keeps missionaries' and other friends'
pictures and prayer requests in a prayer scrapbook, and prays
through it regularly. The family altar is also an ideal time for
teaching such practical, spiritual truths as "how to win other
kids to Christ."

A family will adapt its program to the age of the children, and while they will often have prayers in the language of the country, and include servants or visitors, they will also have, perhaps at bedtime, a special time for the younger children, a time especially suited to them.

Spiritual or even "biblical" training is not to be limited to the family altar, however. Deuteronomy 6:6-9 speaks of the practical outworking of a wholehearted love for God in a parent.

> These words, which I command thee this day, shall be upon thy heart; and thou shalt teach them diligently unto thy children, and shalt talk of them when thou sittest in thy house and when thou walkest by the way, and when thou liest down, and when thou risest up . . . and thou shalt write them upon the door-posts of thy house, and upon thy gates.

Again, in Deuteronomy 6:20-25:

> When thy son asketh thee in time to come, saying, What mean the testimonies, and the statutes, and the ordinances, which Jehovah our God hath commanded you? then thou shalt say unto thy son, We were Pharaoh's bondmen . . . and Jehovah brought us out from thence, . . . And Jehovah commanded us to do all these statutes, to fear Jehovah our God, for our good always, . . ."

All through the day as situations arise, Bible teaching and Bible truth are to be applied to the life, thankfulness and praise are to be stimulated, and actions are to be tested and evaluated on the basis of biblical precepts.

"He whose spirit is without restraint is like a city that is broken down and without walls" (Proverbs 25:28) takes on new meaning to a child when he is learning the verse because he lost his temper. And while fruit may not be seen immediately in the life of a child, a faithful sowing of the seed of God's Word will eventually transform his life.

A teen-age missionary daughter gave cause for thought in the following comment:

> I think this whole thing goes even deeper. Of course, almost all MK's families have "family altar." Almost all MK's are trained in Christian principles and habits—Bible reading, praying, and so on. The problem seems to me to lie in the fact that not enough of us have been taught *WHY* we do these things—what it should mean to us and what it does for us. In other words, I feel some of our parents don't take time to see that we have a genuine experience with the Lord Jesus that blooms into a relationship with Him that makes Bible reading, prayer, and all these Christian principles meaningful. I do have to realize that I've been away from home more than at home since I was nine. These things could be taught from the earliest age, though.
>
> By no means do I want to imply that I feel parents are passing this area over as not so important as their more demanding duties. I believe they earnestly long for this reality of experience to be true in their children. I wonder if maybe some just don't have any idea of how to go about this "child evangelism."

As Ruth Campbell wrote:

> It is most important that the message of the Bible get into the experience of the children at an early age, and that they be aware that their parents find the Bible a resource for their own lives.[8]

Another aspect of early spiritual training is that of church attendance and behavior. Church attendance should be a joyful duty, and it should be taken for granted that all in the family will attend with exceptions made only because of real illness. The reason for this is that Christians are commanded not to forsake the assembling of themselves together (Hebrews 10:25), and this should be explained to the children. Some parents make it a strong point to take all the children to all

---

[8]Ruth N. Campbell, *op. cit.,* p. 32.

the meetings, others feel it may not be wise to keep young children out late at night. However this may be, it *is* extremely important that the children be taught to reverence the house of God, and to be quiet and well-behaved during the services. As children grow older, they may be encouraged to take notes or pick out parts of sermons which can serve for further topics of discussion. Certainly they should be taught not to run, shouting, down the aisles, just because the service has finished. Even tiny children can be taught that they are to be quiet, also that they are not to run around during or after church services.

Church attendance also affords training in giving, and parents should think this through carefully. Should children be trained to give liberally? Perhaps the children should put in the dollar bills while the parents give the nickels. As they grow older and have an allowance, or start earning money, they can be encouraged to give regularly and sacrificially to the Lord of that which is their own.

In all of this, the national church is watching. As they see missionary parents training their children, so will they train theirs. Once again, let me emphasize this: A faithful fulfilling of a family responsibility inadvertently becomes a missionary ministry.

SOCIAL TRAINING

These early years of a child's life are definitely years of social training. For their children's sake, if for no other reason, parents need to keep an open house and open hearts. The need for proper playmates, especially if there are few children in the family, can be urgent and should be prayed about daily. One of a child's greatest assets as he leaves home is a natural, open friendliness and a sincere interest in others.

> Love for all men is not an accident. It is something that is both taught and caught—in the family. It is taught by the conversation and incidental remarks in the

home. It is caught from our attitudes—from interest in missions, from the conception we have of the Church . . . from the presence or absence of missionary books and reading, and from the hundred other things a family does or does not do.[9]

A child's parents must take care to teach him basic social customs, such as correct table manners and proper procedures for greeting or introducing people. These must be learned for both cultures and both should become instinctive to the child.

However, there are certain adaptations to American life that save a missionary child a great deal of heartache and uncertainty, and fit him to take his place easily among his companions in the homeland. Parents can help appreciably along these lines, and so can the mission schools on the field. Boys ought to have a knowledge of sports and perhaps a certain proficiency at them. Girls will need instruction and help in choosing clothes and wearing them, in grooming and care of the hair, in posture, and how to walk and sit. Parents would be foolish to overlook the opportunities such teaching would provide for fellowship and closer mutual understanding with their children.

A missionary's daughter wrote:

I am just beginning to see the importance of a well-rounded experience in the area of social life, the arts, the item of dress. This last applies to parents as well as children. Sometimes the folks don't realize that one way of dressing is acceptable and necessary on the field and another in the States. The MK lacks confidence and a sense of security and acceptance when he is not dressed decently according to the styles. This would make it easier for children going away from home. I have seen how the Lord can provide, and we don't have to look like paupers. Of course, we should understand the difference between material mindedness and dressing nicely

---

[9]Oscar E. Feucht (ed.). *Making Home Life Christian:* Parent Guidance Series No. 2, (St. Louis: Concordia Publishing House, n. d.) p. 42.

to be a pleasing testimony to the Lord Jesus, whom we represent.

D. E. Ralson, in a study related to this one, wrote:

> Missionaries should strive to be informed about the adjustment problems their children must face and be prepared to help them. Parents should tell their children about life in the United States. They should keep as well informed as possible on what the youth of America are doing. . . . The missionary child needs a lot of instruction on boy-girl relationships before leaving home. Help should be given the student not to feel so different.[10]

The facts as presented in this study were worthy of careful note, for, of all problems, those of social adjustment were the greatest. Concerning this type of problem the findings were as follows:

> Out of 34 studies, 6 claimed to have no particular problems, but the remaining 28 mentioned this type of problem 132 times. The most common were adjusting to heterosexual friendships. . . . "I had to learn how to act in front of girls. I'm still learning how to act in front of them." . . . They thought they should at least know how American young people acted, and how they as Christian youth were expected to conduct themselves.[11]

A missionary daughter, now grown and married, wrote at length about this matter:

> MK's have quite a reputation. Some are misfits and come back to the U. S. not knowing how to dress, wearing sloppy mismatching "missionary barrel" clothes. Some have a very noticeable holier-than-thou attitude, partly because they've had a good Christian background and people have led them to think that their parents are the most wonderful people in the earth to deprive them-

---

[10]D. E. Ralson, "The Adjustment Problems of American Students Reared on the Mission Field," unpublished Master's dissertation, Eastern Baptist Theological Seminary, 1949, p. 51.

[11]Ibid., p. 24.

selves and go to the backside of the desert. Some kids have never had other kids their age to play with, have been taught completely by their parents and so have only adjusted to a grown-up world. Some have been stuck away in boarding school and have been moved from place to place until they feel very insecure. This can cause them to be shy introverts or it can make them rebel and want to show the world that they really are worth something. Most of the missionary kids I've known are well-adjusted and above average in intelligence and ability, and for this we praise the Lord. They have had the advantage of travel and of having many people praying for them. But there have been a few misfits—one in the realm of dress, another girl who rebelled and married a Roman Catholic fellow while she was still in school, and a fellow who was a behavior problem in high school.

In my own experience I was very much aware of my parents' prayers and guidance. They gave us principles for conduct but did not impose strict rules on us in high school when we were back in the U.S. I've greatly appreciated this. It taught us to act because we had thought things through for ourselves. Another thing I appreciate is the fact that we were not sheltered from "the world." I've met many MK's who have never been to anything but a Christian school. Most of them would be scared stiff to lead a Bible study or witness to a non-Christian on their own level. They are prepared to do children's work or to work in jails or with derelicts, but are not able to think on the same wavelength as people their own age who are not Christians. Some are so sheltered that it has never occurred to them that there are any intellectual difficulties in believing the Scriptures so they cannot understand, let alone help, anyone who has difficulties. It is understandable that parents who are not able to have as close a relationship or supervision over their children would want to send them somewhere they felt would give them this supervision. However I do feel they should be aware of the danger of growing a hot-

house Christian—one who has never been able to grow
strong because of having adverse winds blow on him.
In my own experience I went one year to Wheaton College and then four years to a State University. The Lord
taught through both places and I wouldn't want to do
without either. Of course, this is not God's plan for
everyone, and we can trust Him to guide each individual
in the very best way for that individual.

While it is important that a child learn to fit in with others,
it is even more important that he learn social independence
and self-respect. And he may not find it emotionally desirable
to conform to the ways of groups with wrong standards. This
comes partly as a result of knowing social customs and being
able to fit in with them, but in greater degree he achieves it as
he measures himself not by others but by what the Lord indicates in the Word. It is assisted by the teaching of his parents
and their joyous acceptance of their place in life. A second-
generation missionary mother wrote:

> My advice to mothers is that they never make their
> children feel they are missing out on lots of things be-
> cause they are missionaries' kids. I was one and have
> always been glad of it. In fact there are lots of advan-
> tages in being an MK!

A missionary's daughter wrote:

> I have often wondered why some MK's regret that
> they are MK's. Maybe it is partly because their parents
> don't take the time to give the proper orientation toward
> and understanding of their privilege. I don't recall my
> folks ever talking about it as such; it just has been an
> atmosphere and an attitude. . . .

A mother who has achieved this in her children wrote:

> I feel my children have been the "gainers," having
> learned another language, another culture, and having
> learned to truly love another people. My oldest daughter

reads all the minutes, letters and papers that come from Venezuela with as much anticipation as we do. She talks about visiting her adopted country frequently. While at school when she came home on weekends she often went into the girls' dorm of the Bible Institute to visit with them before coming into the house to greet us.

ACCEPTANCE OF NATIONALS

All this training has been going on in the presence of the nationals and while the child is coping—daily, in his early years—with a culture that is foreign to his parents but entirely natural to him. It is the parents who experience confusion or frustration, and if they are not careful, they will transfer their feelings to their children. This is an area which often burdens missionary children. Different ones wrote:

> I think that missionary children should be allowed to be identified with the nationals. I have seen parents that try to curtail the contact with the people and the whole foreigner-national relationship is not as full.
>
> Children should be brought up with the knowledge of their own native customs and yet should be allowed to participate in the national culture.
>
> The missionary mother is to a large extent the controller of the child's attitudes, prejudices, and acceptances as far as national people and customs are concerned. She should realize this and take appropriate precautions in her own attitudes, actions, and words.
>
> Children should, of course, be brought up in the Lord, in that country. Actually, our culture is not so good, the only good we have to offer is Jesus Christ.
>
> I was brought up in constant contact with the nationals and I can see very little harm in contrast to the vast benefits . . .
>
> One of the first problems a missionary mother faces is the question of companions or playmates for children on the field. . . . I believe missionary parents whose children mingle with the national children have a better

chance of reaching the hearts of all the people whom
they are trying to reach.

As the parents themselves get their emotional balance and
learn to trust or distrust the nationals, not on the basis of their
being nationals but on the basis of what the Lord has been
able to do in their individual lives, they will be able to encourage their children to a complete acceptance of the national. This is easy to the child if he is not taught otherwise, and
it is essential to the full effectiveness of the missionary parents'
ministry. A child's attitudes toward those of other races reflect what he has been taught, consciously or unconsciously,
by others. Occasionally a missionary child will react with a
rather fierce resentment against the "foreigners" (Americans)
who dare to look down upon the people among whom he lives.

On the other hand, parents must also be on the alert to
detect snobbishness of any kind in their youngsters, especially
when there are other missionary children around. All missionary children must always show all courtesy to the nationals
and the utmost respect—and these are qualities the missionaries themselves do well to cultivate.

This sudden acquisition of "superiority" is one of the
problems that must be faced in connection with children's
schooling on the field. Since children absorb so quickly the
prejudices of fellow students or teachers, this respect for the
national is a qualification that houseparents and other personnel for children's schools must foster carefully, both in themselves and in their young charges.

DANGERS

However, there is another danger that is likely to overtake
the missionary child on the field when there is a close relationship between the missionary and the nationals—contracting
a contagious disease. In most foreign countries there is no
isolation of cases of measles, smallpox, whooping cough or
other more serious diseases, and many, many beloved little
folk have paid with their lives for their parents' obedience to

the missionary call. Can we blame a mother for becoming overprotective with her children? Mrs. Jonathan Goforth told of her husband's asking her to go out with him on country tours of evangelism:

> Yes, it was a very wonderfully thought-out plan and should be carried out IF there were no children in the question!
>
> As I listened, my heart went like lead! The vision of those women with their smallpox children at Hotsun, crowding about me and the baby, the constant danger to the children from all kinds of infectious diseases that this life would mean, (for the Chinese cared nothing of bringing infection to others), and the thought of our four little graves,—all combined to make me set my face as adamant against the plan. My one and only reason, however, in opposing and refusing to go with my children, as my husband suggested, was because it seemed a risking of the children's lives.
>
> Oh how my husband pleaded! . . . He said:
>
> "Rose, I am so sure this plan is of God, that I fear for the children if you refuse to obey His call. *The safest place for you and the children is the path of duty.* You think you can keep the children safe in your comfortable home at Changte, but God may have to show you you cannot. But He can and will keep the children if you trust Him and step out in faith!"
>
> [After this, baby Wallace became seriously ill.]
>
> For two weeks we literally fought for the child's life during which my husband whispered to me gently, "Oh, Rose, give in, before it is too late!" But I only thought him hard and cruel, and refused.[12]

Douglas Sargent has commented:

> And what wonderful little missionaries the children sometimes are, with their natural gifts for friendliness and their ability to set strangers at ease! But it is easy to

---

[12]Rosalind Goforth, *Goforth of China* (Grand Rapids: Zondervan Publishing House, 1937) p. 156-58.

be over-sentimental at this point. Let no one imagine, despite all the joy they bring, that children make life easier on the mission field for their parents. It is not merely that they are time-consuming, as they are any-where in the world, but that the wise parent has at the same time to encourage the child to play with other chil-dren of a different race, and also to safeguard the child's health in conditions often by no means hygienic. The over-anxious parent will soon find that the child is be-coming not a means of contact with others but a cause of withdrawal from them.[13]

It is a matter that calls for great heartsearching. "He that would save his life shall lose it." How much more risk does a mother run when she grasps as her own the lives of little ones loaned to her by God—especially when she is powerless to protect them anyway! Is it hard to believe that His love for them is wiser and more perfect than hers?

Gracie, the lovely little daughter of Dr. and Mrs. Hudson Taylor, died of encephalitis at the age of eight years.

"Who plucked this flower?" said the gardener.

"The Master," answered his fellow workman. And the gardener held his peace.[14]

If there is one thing we dare not keep to ourselves, it is our loved ones. On the other hand, it is the mother's responsi-bility to safeguard her children in every possible way. She will teach them to keep their hands out of their mouths. She will feed them as wholesome a diet as possible and watch over their eating, drinking, and sleeping habits. She will see to it that their shots and immunizations are kept up to date. She will patiently instruct them and the people in matters of hygiene. And then she will simply trust the Lord.

There is one truly serious danger to which parents must be alerted. Their children are growing up in a land given over to

---

[13]Douglas N. Sargent, *op. cit.*, p. 120.
[14]Dr. and Mrs. Howard Taylor, *Hudson Taylor and the China Inland Mission* (London: The China Inland Mission, 1927) p. 118.

sin and idolatry, and even the Christians are still often tainted with the trappings of the "old man."

As the missionary children grew up, the problem of their relationship to the native children is often a very live one. If they are allowed to play with them, unless it is very carefully supervised, there is a very real danger of their picking up all sorts of unclean words and practices, which are characteristic of nearly all children in mission fields. Some who have grown up as missionary children and who were allowed to "run with the pack" have expressed their conviction that it is only by an act of supernatural grace that they were kept from remembering and becoming enslaved to some of the unwholesome practices which they had learned while young.[15]

Unceasing vigilance on the part of the parents is ever the price of purity in the children, and many sorrowing fathers and mothers both in Christian and non-Christian lands have awaked to find that while they were busy here and there about good and useful tasks, their children's purity was gone, they knew not how.[16]

Don't build a wall around them. They will be a testimony on the field. They will learn the language quickly. They can attract national children. Don't take the position that your children are too good to associate with national children.

Protect them from the evil influences of a degraded society. While you should not keep them entirely aloof, neither should you let them run wild. They can easily pick up bad language and bad habits from national children. Exercise reasonable control and supervision over them.[17]

A second-generation missionary mother wrote:

[15] T. Stanley Soltau (Grand Rapids: Baker Book House, 1959), p. 102.
[16] Annie L. Baird, *Inside Views of Mission Life* (Philadelphia: Westminster Press, 1913), pp. 55-56.
[17] *Baptist Mid-Missions' Principles and Practices.* Candidate Seminar Manual No. 1. (Cleveland, Ohio: n.d.), n.p.

We have never let the children just "run" with the national children, but if they have been together have them at home where one knows what they are doing. Some kids have been left without their parents' knowing the habits and language they were learning. Also, I never felt that it was right to leave children with servants when they were small. In Latin America at times servants are careless or teach them sinful habits.

This is a greater danger than some realize, and it does require constant, quiet vigilance and faithful, earnest prayer on the part of the missionary parents. Second-generation missionaries are particularly conscious of this, and it could explain the fact, indicated in the questionnaire responses and other sources, that these tend to care for their children more themselves rather than leaving them regularly to the care of servants. On the other hand, the only real protection is found in the Lord's gracious care for the life of the child. This is worth praying for.

SCHOOLING

The schooling of children, while much less difficult now than forty or even thirty years ago, is still one of the major problems facing the missionary family. Where to send the child, when to send him, how to prepare him—all are considerations to be diligently prayed about and thought through. But today few parents experience the terrible suffering that was the common lot of missionaries of other years, when children often had to be left in the States for schooling at an early age. There was such painful risk involved, both in finding the proper place in which to leave the child, and in trusting him to whatever educational and spiritual influences might strike him during the several years before his parents should see him again. A mother described this:

> . . . Every happy time together was colored with the thought of the coming separation. Their personal needs and a parent's own ambitions for them rise up into the

mind to fog faith, the cross and the call to missionary service. Will someone else stand in the gap to meet the child's physical, spiritual, and material needs? Did not Christ say, ". . . he that loveth son or daughter more than me is not worthy of me"? . . . As I look at it now I faced the leaving of the children "as a lamb being led to slaughter." I did not know the victory I learned in later years when I left eight children instead of two. If others could do it for Christ's sake, I could too.

Comparatively few mothers teach their own children nowadays beyond the first grade or two (though this can be done easily with the Calvert course, or other correspondence courses), but neither is it often necessary to send young children away to the States for school at such an early age. Whoever teaches the child, his schooling should begin at the normal age, if possible; and he should not leave home until he is established in every area of personality. This emotional and spiritual readiness will come sooner or later as the parents pray and train him.

Early home schooling is not difficult, but it does require faithfulness and self-discipline on the part of the mother. It can be a rewarding experience to open to the child the field of letters, but it should also be a stimulating experience for the child. If he does not learn to enjoy study in the first and second grades, he is likely to be handicapped all his life. While correspondence courses are somewhat expensive, they are well planned, and the parents can be confident that their children are receiving an adequate education as long as the children handle the work without undue assistance from their teacher. School at home lacks the competition experienced in large classes, but it gives ample opportunity to master a subject in less time.

The comments of different missionary children on this subject showed the interest MK's take in their own problem. For instance a second generation missionary pointed up a noticeable trend:

I wonder if you wouldn't find MK's feel a bit stronger about trying to keep their children as close as possible and as long as possible. The other families now on our station send their children to a missionary children's home 100 miles away and see them rather infrequently. We sent our first daughter there at six and saw her so seldom. Then when the second girl was about to start at five and a half, we investigated a government boarding school (eighteen miles away) and sent our girls there for over two years until furlough. True, they didn't have the Christian environment, but were home *three* nights a week (every weekend) and at school four nights each week. We'd do it again if we were stationed there, for we never had tears at partings, nor did they or we lose contact with each other.

Others (not MK's) however, feel the sheltered Christian environment of our Children's Home more important than having them home every weekend. And I think my own MK life influences my thinking on the subject! I was home until 10 years of age, then was 300 miles away most of the rest of the time. And I still feel it best to have our children home if at all possible in the earlier years especially.

EVENTUAL SEPARATION

However, the separation does come eventually, and wise parents will condition the child for it from an early age. They should not dwell on it mournfully, especially before the child, but rather speak of it happily and matter-of-factly, taking it for granted that the child is satisfied about it. The family should pray about it together and separately, and the Lord will prepare the child and lead as to the place for study. It is always good if a child can know some of the children or teachers before he goes, or at least have visited the place on some occasion.

The actual parting need not be difficult for the child. If the parents have prepared him for it, and if he senses that they are satisfied before the Lord that this is His will, he is likely to accept it easily. For the parent there is always the strength of the Lord. A mother of several children wrote:

> For the separations I always find that when the time comes, the grace comes, though there are many times of desolation. I feel that is so we can see what the Lord is keeping us from, and then when we cry to Him, He does it again, and on we go, quite normal again.

The really hard part is having to hand over to the care and training of others a child whom the parents so deeply love, in spite of his faults. The qualities they have been building in his life seem as yet hardly more than embryonic, and yet they feel that he is being cast out where they can no longer reach him. The mother finds it is *she* who needs the weaning process, not her child. It seems almost impossible, but from now on, for the child's best good, the parents must not interfere with others' handling of their children. They should work closely with the teachers and houseparents of the school and trust them. If parents disagree with the care and teaching of their child, they should not let the child know their feelings. At times like this, it is a very real comfort to put both child and the situation in the Lord's hands. One very sensible mother wrote:

> Perhaps my children are more independent at an earlier age. I've listened to complaints about boarding school but I always minimize them and feel it will blow over. Of course I pray much! Now that we are home on furlough my two oldest speak often of their good times, special food, and happy occasions. I praise the Lord because they show no resentments and have adjusted very well to Stateside living.

The kind of cooperation houseparents and school authorities appreciate is indicated by the following points:

1. Write often, lovingly, and happily.
2. Do not undermine discipline, however you feel about it.

Express yourself reasonably but courteously to the school authorities.

3.   Visit as the school permits, but not oftener.

4.   When visiting, firmly uphold the rules of the school.

The readjustment to home life takes some thought. Parents must allow time for the child to settle into the home routine. They should take every possible opportunity while the child is back home to show how glad they are that he's home. They can do this by planning fun and fellowship of all kinds, and by conversation in which they share experiences and points of view. A mother wrote:

> We have tried to do things with the children when they are home—to go on hikes, picnics, and so on. I have always read stories to them at bedtime. Even though they have had to be away from home for seven months of the year since they were six years old, I have always made them feel that I have missed them, and would rather have them at home if it were for the best. We always made partings as easy as possible, not hanging onto the children and mourning the fact that they had to go away. We encouraged each to do his best in school according to his individual ability.

Another said:

> I feel that it is very important to enter wholeheartedly into whatever you are doing with the children. They are quick to sense it if your mind is elsewhere, and there's not too much comfort in your physical presence, if it's limited to that. Separation time comes all too soon, and you want their hearts well stocked with memories of good times of doing things together.

During the time at home, however, discipline should in no way be relaxed. It must remain loving and firm, and truth and obedience must always be required. These times together are for mutual delight, but the child is still immature, and his training must continue.

Letter-writing is of major importance during children's absences. One mother wrote:

> I have written to them twice a week, trying to write about things that are interesting to children—not adult interests. Those letters have meant much to them. I have seen children whose folks hardly wrote because they were so busy in the Lord's work, or when they did, they wrote all about how they had been sick or were tired, or all about the adult work they were doing.

It is good if fathers also write occasionally.
One MK wrote:

> . . . I began to realize that I had not heard from Daddy in a long time. . . . It was seeming more and more like my letters were just addressed to Mom in answer to hers, though I did start it "Dear Mommy, Daddy, and girls," . . . In the next letter I asked Daddy to write sometime, as I felt I was losing contact with him somehow. Of course he answered. In the letter he said he had considered his "Home Folks" carbon copies as something from him to me. I do feel the fathers should write every month or so to make the children feel just as much loved by them as by the mother. After this little incident it was *so* good of the Lord to make it possible for me to spend ten days with Daddy at Christmas time.

And this is what another missionary daughter wrote about letters:

> One very important thing to me now as an MK separated from my parents for an extended period of time is the knowledge that I am still loved very much and that I am missed, especially by my mother. My mother is very busy, I know, and yet she writes twice a week to me and to my brother at Wheaton. It means so much to me, since I know she loves to do it and doesn't just do it because she feels she must.

Both in letters and in the times when parents are with

their children, they should seek to encourage them in the Lord, to help them see God's purpose in hard or discouraging experiences, and to challenge each one to follow after God's own best for his life.

This early separation is bound to pose problems, but no child is beyond the reach of God Who hears prayer. A child who feels neglected can be loved back to acceptance of his lot. God can work a miracle in the heart of the rebellious child. One mother felt that early separation may tend to work for early marriage. There is always the danger of a child's choosing wrong paths and needing to be brought back. Parents experience the undeniable disappointment, as children get older, of missing graduations and weddings and rarely seeing grandchildren; but the God of all comfort is sufficient for each one.

The heart of the matter was expressed in a letter from Dr. Henry Brandt, the Christian psychologist:

> The best way to prepare a child for absence from a parent is to maintain a wholesome, friendly relationship with that child. In talking to children who have been away from their parents, I find the ones that make a satisfactory adjustment alone are those who have come from a stable, happy home—this is the best preparation that you can have for a child who needs to be away from home.

This is how a missionary daughter said the same thing:

> I think that the children should know in their hearts that their mother belongs to them, that her time is their time, and that she is not too busy, even in the Lord's work, for them and their problems. The children should be made to feel free to confide in their parents. Otherwise, they will tend to go around in a world of their own and will not heed the instruction and discipline from their parents as they should. How can the teaching of the home make the impact it should upon a child who really doesn't know his parents and feels that they don't care

about or understand him anyway? Of course, the parents shouldn't spoil them or indulge them, nor allow the nationals to do this. But I believe that they shouldn't get so involved in their work that the children get the feeling that they kind of have to take care of themselves and solve their own problems. I don't know what I would have done had I not had parents to whom I could go when I wanted to and who had not been genuinely interested in me.

We may conclude, then, that love, coupled with availability, discipline, and instruction, provides the physical setting in which our children are taught of God; and that He does this in answer to prayer.

A missionary mother was kneeling in prayer one morning when two tiny hands reached for her face and pulled it over to look straight into two brown eyes.

"Mother, are you praying?" the child asked.

"Yes, Honey," the mother answered, and went back to prayer.

Again the little hands reached for her face, and the brown eyes looked searchingly into hers.

"Mother, are you praying for me?"

That mother will never forget the joy of intercession for her own.

CHAPTER 4

HER HOME

The modern Protestant missionary movement is a family movement, in contrast to the celibate personnel sent by the Roman Catholic church. Missionary couples comprise a large proportion of the Protestant force and today there are at least 10,000 children of North American missionary families in the range between babyhood and college age. The education of these children is an important phase of Protestant missionary work, and the homes in which they are being reared are at the center of the missionary program.[1]

THE HOME is the special pulpit of the missionary mother. In a sense it is the final proof to the world that the Gospel presented by the missionary is more than a doctrine or a concept: it is a life.

For this reason, it can be affirmed that when a missionary mother runs her home smoothly and lives in it exemplarily, she is not just serving her husband and children or satisfying her own conscience; she is giving a clear demonstration of the outworkings of the Gospel in everyday life.

A minister's wife once described life in a parsonage like being "in a goldfish bowl."

> When you begin life in a parsonage, you and your family become the goldfish inside the parsonage bowl. The onlookers are the parishioners who love to gaze and

[1]Clara E. Orr, "The Education of Missionaries' Children" *Occasional Bulletin* from the Missionary Research Library (3041 Broadway, New York, N. Y.), Vol. X, No. 9 (Nov. 10, 1959), p. 1.

exaggerate the parson's family. Every detail of your life is going to be known and what isn't known is imagined. How often you will wonder why it looks so golden and rosy to the onlookers!

Like the goldfish you, too, are imported, . . . You and your family, ordinary carp, to be sure, have a special glow because of the curiosity and publicity which surround you; and you cannot avoid exposure to the public gaze.[2]

A MISSIONARY MINISTRY

The words seem to fit the missionary situation exactly; especially in primitive or pioneer areas. They express precisely the reason a woman need waste no tears over the hours she cannot spend doing "missionary work." As a wife and mother she is not *telling* people how a Christian acts at home; she is *showing* them. For this reason she must allow the Lord to be, in very truth, Lord of her life and of her home.

She dare not permit any resentment toward the people at the lack of privacy that is often her portion. She has gone to live among them in order to have contact with them to reach them with the Gospel, and while in time she *will* try tactfully to give her husband a certain amount of privacy that he can better accomplish his ministry, she must never do so by building barriers. The love of God alone will enable her to do this tactfully.

Her own chief area of contact with the nationals will be in her home, especially while her children are young. Depending on the circumstances of each case, of course, much of her actual missionary work will be done within the four walls of her home. If she is a true missionary, with a heart reaching out to minister to the needs of all about her, she will find this an ample field and a fruitful one.

On the other hand, the missionary mother may find that household duties can completely entangle her, and she will

---

[2]Welthy Honsinger Fisher, *Handbook for Ministers' Wives* (New York: Woman's Press, 1950), p. 23.

wonder seriously if she has any ministry at all. It is with this possibility in view that this study has attempted to go behind the scenes to simplify the problem.

If the questionnaires can be considered valid for drawing such conclusions, the average missionary mother spends roughly one third to one half of her time on housework. This study covered eighty-nine families ranging from two with no children (included as an interesting control element) to one with a grown family of eleven children, several of them serving on the foreign field. Several more mothers contributed material in interviews, and these findings were incorporated with those of the questionnaires, so that the total number of mothers reached one hundred.

There was only one mother whose housework occupied her full time with a servant. She was housemother for twenty children, but further examination of her answers revealed that she also helps with children's classes and radio work.

The amount of time required for housework is controlled, predictably, by several factors. The number of children a mother has at home runs the figure up or down. The presence of servant help and/or conveniences greatly reduces the time involved. How much organizational and homemaking skill the mother herself has is the truly determining factor. Her health enters into this last, of course, for limited strength inevitably curtails one's physical output.

FLEXIBILITY

Houses on the mission field run the entire gamut from the absolutely primitive to the most ultramodern, beautifully furnished homes. Oddly enough, in the course of her missionary career, a woman may preside over several types of "mansions," moving easily from parquet flooring to mud-and-thatch and back to cement-and-tin, sometimes at short notice. Whatever her situation, she will find her housekeeping must be subject to the laws of flexibility, diligence, and careful organization. Of wisdom, which she needs constantly, her Lord offers a liberal supply. And He will be teaching her, in whatever state she is, to be content.

The first law, then, is flexibility. This is partly a mental attitude, but it is developed by the acceptance of moving situations. If she moves often, the woman will study ways to simplify the packing involved. She will learn to determine what items will be most useful for minimum living and will, over a period of years, establish her own list of "essentials." But the frustration over constant moves, especially with young children, can be overcome only by acceptance of them as from the Lord. The battle is not easy, as a missionary with five children wrote to her mother recently:

> Dear Mother:
> Just a line this evening. Had a real nice "pre-Christmas dinner" yesterday and then we all opened presents. Missed you not being here. I spent all morning packing to leave tomorrow. Glen came home and announced everything is closed up till Monday. More fun. This evening I unpack *again*. What is the Lord trying to teach me? I've spent nearly the whole week *packing* and *unpacking* and still have some to go. Then out to Chinimbi next week to *unpack* and *pack up* to send stuff to Shell. Then to Limón to *unpack*. Hah! As Esther says, "Maybe you better just start liking it." Up to now I don't. . . .

Especially must this attitude of flexibility apply to the use of conveniences and/or servant help. If she has them, she uses them; if she doesn't, she does without; and she learns to make the change with comparative ease.

Housekeeping conditions can vary on the field, according to one's location. In some primitive situations a woman will need to have all water brought from the river or pond some distance away, and will take the family wash down to the river and do it there just as the other ladies about her do (if they do a wash!). She may cook on a wood fire with her pans set on three stones. Obviously her housekeeping problems are simplified to a degree. She never has to worry about dusting venetian blinds or waxing floors. One missionary mother laughed merrily as she showed off her jungle home to her visiting sister. "These split chonta floors have one real advantage," she said. "You never have to mop up spills!" Still, thanks to missionary aviation, even jungle kitchens occasionally see packages of cake mix.

A missionary mother wrote very graphically about a station she and her husband moved to:

> My husband preceded me to the station and built a mud hut 14 x 14 ft. for our temporary quarters until the mission house could be built. The place we used for a kitchen was a grass mat shelter, three stones to cook on, and a kerosene tin banked with mud to use for an oven to make bread. To me, these were thrills of adventure. The area was being cleared of stones and brush. Already my husband had killed a six-foot-long cobra. There were scorpions . . . dust storms and hot dry winds in the dry season; heavy rain storms in the rainy season and we had little protection. I recall that my husband and I braced all our strength against a grass mat covering for our window to try to keep out the wind and rain during a terrific storm.

In a houseful of children, few would question the couplet,

> Man's work is from sun to sun,
> But woman's work is never done.

Ordinarily, the work of a missionary is a full-time job by itself. Likewise the work of housewife-mother is full-time. Just how necessary is it that a missionary mother take time from "missionary work" to keep her house clean and running smoothly? A pastor's wife put it this way:

> If a woman feels she ought to leave her house in disorder and dirt while she does "work for the Lord," she has a dislocated sense of duty. If a woman cannot render such service without neglecting her home and family,

then let the claims of the home come first. Before she looks elsewhere for openings to do good, let her set her own house in order. After guests have come and gone, whether or not she knew of their coming, may she hear the voice of the Lord whispering: "What have they seen in thy house?"[3]

Another wrote:

Be it ever so humble, your parsonage can be clean. A broom, mop, pail, and box of detergent, plus an ample supply of elbow grease, can transform any dingy parsonage into a sparkling set of rooms. Keeping the woodwork and windows clean, the furniture in order and the toys picked up is a matter of bodily exercise, which the Apostle Paul says is profitable.

The habitual appearance of dirty dishes in the midst of an unkept kitchen is inexcusable. Parish duties should never come ahead of parsonage obligations. Your first responsibility is to provide a clean, well-ordered home for your pastor-husband and your family.[4]

For the missionary wife in a primitive setting, her attitude to the children and their behavior would be more important than the state of the household, but she cannot teach cleanliness and care of the family without practicing it.[5]

Housekeeping on the mission field includes and takes for granted many processes that in the homeland are for the most part unknown. In the ordinary American home the mother will use an eggbeater and immediately rinse it off under the faucet so it will be easy to wash. If she needs to use it again, she uses it. Not so in the ordinary missionary home. If there is running water in the kitchen—and there may or may not be—she may rinse the eggbeater, but she won't use it again until soap and boiling water have done their work. Depending on the

---

[3]Carolyn P. Blackwood, *The Pastor's Wife* (Philadelphia: The Westminster Press, 1951), p. 47.
[4]Lora Lee Parrott, *How to be a Preacher's Wife and Like It* (Grand Rapids: Zondervan Publishing House, 1956), pp. 44-45.
[5]Eunice Pike, *Women Chosen by the Lord,* pamphlet published by Wycliffe Bible Translators, Glendale, California, p. 5.

heat, the size of her family, and the number of guests, she will boil between two and eight or more gallons of water for ten to twenty minutes, as required in the particular area where they live. (A timer, incidentally, is a marvelous aid to accurately time the boiling of water.) Then she may filter this boiled water and, if she can, put some of it in the refrigerator.

If she is going to cook rice, she will first pick it over carefully to remove small bits of stone, or brush, or weevils, and/or small white worms.

If she is going to use lettuce or other raw things for salad, she will often need to soak them first in a solution of potassium permanganate or dilute Clorox, and then wash them repeatedly (in boiled water, of course).

When she buys meat (probably by the hunk), she will look it over and decide what its possibilities are. If she wants to make hamburgers or meat loaf, she will get out her grinder and, after removing as much gristle as possible, will grind the meat.

It's amazing what a woman can do in case of need. One mother told of an unusual birthday cake which she had made:

> For our boy's third birthday we were far out in a village. I made a steamed chocolate pudding which I cooled and frosted to delight him for his birthday. This was prepared over the three stones as I squatted in African fashion in a native's compound.

The illustrations are infinite and, of course, conditions vary from place to place. Still, a mother must learn just how much strength she can afford to give in answer to some of the really hard physical demands of such living. One such mother wrote:

> Before coming on furlough I had done my own family washing for two years on a scrub board. I thought I was saving money and the "trouble" of having another servant. Now I realize it was a mistake, for I lost weight and broke out with sores—just plain run down. Hope my lesson has been learned.

A mother must also learn to adjust her housework to her physical strength and missionary duties. One woman wrote:

> Too many mothers try to do all they did in the U.S.A., even though learning a new language, a new people, and a new culture. One mother I know won't give up her habit of baking Old World dainties, her own bread, and so on, every few days; and with the added burden of living in a foreign land she has become an absolute witch of a woman—screeching at her children, nagging at her husband, telling off her hired help and in general making everyone miserable. Mothers should be aware of these limitations.

The point is that, for the most part, missionary housekeeping is time-consuming and can also take much of a woman's strength. Add to this a temperamental stove, an insufficient income, and children and people constantly underfoot, and the stage is set for trouble unless the Lord helps her to get her situation in perspective, and He will do just that.

SERVANTS

One of the partial solutions is servant help, at least for long, time-consuming duties, such as rice-picking, washing, or ironing. After all, the task of balancing the missionary mother's duties is largely a matter of time and strength. Therefore anything that will save time and strength without otherwise complicating the situation is a wise and a sensible thing to do— if one can afford it. For instance, the mother quoted first in this chapter solved her problem in this fashion:

> We had servants to help with the cooking and cleaning of the house and to take the baby out in his carriage to relieve me for station work, or to be on guard while the baby was sleeping in his bed. We had no household appliances. We used a wood stove, had no Fridge or electric lights, had no car. We used bicycles for distance travel or trekking.

Another mother put it this way:

> I have trained the houseboys to carry most of the work,
> since our living conditions, while not primitive exactly,
> require time and strength. They can't do what I do, that
> is, teaching and translating, but they can be taught
> housework and are looked up to because of that accom-
> plishment. Our home life is a great influence on them and
> their family life.

It may be stated that a missionary hardly takes a servant
because she likes to have service. Servants can be a dreadful
nuisance and a great frustration. They often do their work
poorly (and must be taught), and they may be sticky-fingered
or loose-tongued. Many a missionary home or cupboard has
been rifled by a dishonest servant. Servants with low morals
can contaminate the children who live in the home. Then there
will be days when for some inexplicable reason a servant finds
it inconvenient to report to work. Inevitably these will be
days when help is urgently needed. One missionary mother
wrote: "This seems where most grace is needed—with a
maid. We say, 'Maids worketh patience.' "

But then, that is only one side of the situation. There are
missionaries who have reported servants who were "a delight
—a part of our family, fine Christians. Their work was wonderful."

If a missionary mother needs servant help, she can ask the
Lord for His choice of a servant. This is worth praying about.
Then she can accept that servant complete with good and bad
characteristics. From now on, the servant is included in the
close family circle to whom the mother ministers. And such
a ministry is a real one. Often the servant meets with the
family for morning prayers in the native language. One of
the mothers listed in her day's activities private reading and
prayer with the maid.

A pioneer missionary mother, now retired, wrote of various
servants who had helped her through the years:

We always tried to get some help in the house, but some of the women we employed were more of a problem than a help. Some we could not direct because we were so limited in use of the language. In the interior where we worked most of our time on the field, I was quite fortunate with some of the cases.

One girl came to me looking for work. She was only fourteen years old, and I hesitated very much to take her in, but decided to try her out. Eventually I had her for eight years, in two periods. She was willing and apt to learn. She developed wonderfully in the kitchen and household duties. She learned to bake and became an excellent cook. She learned other crafts also, like crocheting, tatting, dressmaking, and what have you. But she was entirely illiterate. After some time, when she had developed so well in the kitchen work, she got a desire to learn to read the Bible (she attended our Sunday school and church services from the beginning), so I offered to teach her to read. I took a half hour after our school was dismissed afternoons to teach her, but was she slow in that line! I thought she would never learn, but I kept on. She often felt discouraged, too, but made up her mind that she *had to learn.* How happy we both were when she could make out some simple words, and from then on she got ahead. The writing was another hurdle to conquer, and then some little arithmetic. She was converted and baptized and joined the church before she left me to do good work in a church in another part of our field. She eventually married a colporteur and helped him much in his work.

Other girls that I had—one six years, another three years, and some shorter times—did not leave my employ without having been taught to read and write and take part in our devotions around the breakfast table. That is an important part of our missionary work. Their story is different from the one I have given you in detail. How I wish I could talk to you!

Even from the point of view of immediate needs, a servant can be a great blessing. Of the mothers studied, roughly two thirds had servants most of the time. Of the other third, four-teen had no servants at all. Several of these last mentioned that their housework took well over half of their time. "Most of it, if it's done well," wrote one. Another considered the question "difficult to answer, as I never get my work done."

On the other hand, the women with part-time help spent approximately the same time on housework as the ones with full-time help. The number of children (above two) did not seem to increase the time perceptibly. Even the part-time help made an enormous difference in the amount of work a woman is set free to do. One mother of four wrote:

> We had servants over the years, sometimes for half a day, sometimes all day and living in with us. When the children were small they were a great help, but as they grew bigger we appreciated more the privacy and felt the children needed to learn to help. We definitely didn't like the live-in situation because our house wasn't made for it and we had no privacy. But we found having a girl to do cleaning and buying in the morning very helpful.

However, even this takes thought, for a servant is only use-ful in proportion to how well trained he or she is. One mis-sionary wrote very explicitly about this matter. Asked what proportion of her time it took to run her house, she said,

> Very little when we have servant help, which is most of the time. I am a strong believer in using servant help for cooking. *All* of the nine girls that I have had in eleven years on the field have learned to cook well in less than a month (only one or two had cooked American food previously) and quickly learned to make bread, pies, cakes, cookies, and can applesauce and preserves and jams of all kinds. Also, after two or three months, all have planned the family menus (well-balanced) every day. It's all a matter of showing them the first few days

and *letting* them do it thereafter. Three of these girls did not know how to read, but either memorized the recipes, or would remember them after a review of them each time. With cooking taking so long on the mission field, where servant help is available I feel it should be used first of all for that. Servants have never cared for our children other than an hour or so at a time, when I had to be out of the house.

Even supposing this mother to be an unusually skilled teacher, all should be challenged to invest time and thought in training servants in the home. Such an investment pays off, and in time a woman recognizes it. A mother of four now entering their teens wrote:

> Just occasionally did I have servant help. With all the children we all had our chores. However, if I had to do it over again, I would try to train one. That was my big trouble . . . I couldn't stay with them to teach them. With a family, I believe it is best if the servant does not "live in." One of my best girls was a lady in her forties. This seemed to work better than one of my own teen-agers' age.

One other great advantage of having a servant in the home is that it provides a close link with the people themselves. Mr. Soltau, who was quoted in earlier chapters, wrote:

> . . . The right kind of servants, trained by the missionaries, are a tremendous help in the home, especially when they are Christians. They carry on the heavier household duties, assist and give hints to the hostess in receiving strangers and visitors, and often introduce household words to the missionary which ordinarily do not come up in regular language classes or in language school.[6]

On the other hand, servants are also a window through which the people look at the missionary very closely.

[6]T. Stanley Soltau, *Facing the Field* (Grand Rapids: Baker Book House, 1959), p. 101.

The servants, of course, regale their friends with every detail of the life of the foreigners that may be of interest to their friends and their families—the way the missionaries train and discipline their children, their attitude toward each other, toward their servants, and toward others—all are most fascinating topics for gossip and conversation! In fact, the missionary's reputation, to a large degree, will depend upon his servants and the kind of reports they spread concerning him and his family. In many cases these faithful helpers come to consider themselves as part of the family circle, and family prayers should be conducted daily with them that they too may grow in the doctrine.[7]

One of the missionary mothers wrote, "Having help in the home gives me the opportunity to know well one or two nationals." While this is true, and can make for mutual blessing, it is well to use it also to point out one caution-sign. Appreciation and even fellowship with one's servants does not mean intimacy, either in sharing of problems or plans. A woman will save that for her husband and the Lord.

The servant situation appears to be changing drastically in several countries. Servants are increasingly difficult to obtain, and wages are becoming very high; as a result, even the nationals are using fewer servants in their homes. Several mothers spoke of this expressly.

Since returning for our third term (all our children were born in this land), I have had only two days of help per week for three or four months. When our children were very small I had full-time help much of the time. As the youngsters are able, more and more, to take care of themselves and help with the housework, we are glad to have as little help as possible. And there are fewer and fewer who want to do maid work at any price.

For these reasons and others, the missionary mother may find it necessary or wise to cut down on the amount of servant

---

[7] *Ibid.*

help she might otherwise use. Still her home must be cared for. She looks then for other time-and-strength-savers, including appliances that she may not have used before.

> Realizing that help would be expensive, and feeling that we would not want more than a minimum of maid service, we brought back both a washer and a dryer. Twelve or thirteen years ago such appliances would have been looked upon as luxuries by the Japanese, but they produce very little comment now. In fact, their only wonder has been why we don't own a T. V. The washer is my lifesaver. With a rather poor back and large laundries, this one item has been worth already about one half of a helper in the home. I use the dryer only when weather does not permit drying outside; electricity is rather expensive.

Actually there is no special virtue in doing without all modern conveniences. It is neither heroic nor sensible unless there is a reason for doing so. Because they can be such a blessing to a busy mother, their use will be considered next.

APPLIANCES

Some missionaries are reluctant to possess and use appliances. The reasons are valid, perhaps, and certainly they should be considered. The following quotations present four different arguments against the use of appliances:

1. I have very few appliances. I dare not get used to them here because we want to be ready to go to the unreached.

2. We live on a much higher plane than they do when they're so poor. We shouldn't even have a gasoline washing machine. They don't. They come from all around to see it when we use it.

3. Appliances break or get out of order, and they take time to fix.

4. We feel that since the nationals are not used to

modern conveniences, it would take more of our time
to supervise their use.

Household appliances have none of the disadvantages of
servants. They do not steal "silver" nor carry off clothes. They
do not require careful training, and they are ready for work
at any time of day or night. They do not corrupt the morals
of children nor gossip about the family. Some appliances
simplify living to such an extent that they actually do away
with some of the greater frustrations of household manage-
ment on the field.

While some appliances require the expenditure of a considerable sum of money, there are times when (prorated over
the time of their predictable, trouble-free usefulness) they may
be an economy. It is possible to "pay" them wages in a savings
account for replacing them when their work is done. If enough
electricity is available, the range of appliances from which one
may choose is almost limitless.

Granted that appliances can be a boon to the missionary
mother, especially when she has no servant help, there is need
to establish criteria by which to choose or rule out appliances.
These are well suggested by the quotations mentioned above.

1. A missionary dares not become dependent upon appliances. If she cannot freely do without them so as
   to serve in more difficult places, it is better not to have
   them; for they are a hindrance to her.

      This situation is unnecessary and uncalled-for. Should
   a missionary's heart ever become dependent on "things,"
   she must immediately correct her attitude before the
   Lord. No *thing* must ever be allowed to stand between
   her and her Lord's will.

2. She must not permit appliances to separate her from
   the people. However, it has been noted that the separation is effected not so much by the possession of a
   few appliances as by the attitude of the missonary toward appliances and people. A missionary must aban-

don all grasping, overprotective attitudes toward things and must learn to live naturally and openly before the people.

3. Missionaries should take to the field only good quality appliances in good condition; otherwise the husbands will be spending an undue amount of time (which they could well use otherwise) repairing or rebuilding "time-saving" conveniences. This is especially true if the husband lacks mechanical experience, which is so often the case.

4. A missionary should weigh the relative value of appliances which for practical reasons demand that they be used personally, thus adding to her duties rather than releasing her from them. It is not difficult, however, to teach a good servant to use appliances intelligently and even to take pride in keeping them in good condition.

5. The selection of appliances depends upon four considerations: the saving of time, of health, of strength, and of expense.

If the missionary mother has to do much of the housework —and this is becoming increasingly the case—the choice of appliances becomes very important. In the study, the mothers were asked to list those which they considered to be most effective in saving of time and conservation of health and strength.

Two appliances, the refrigerator and the washing machine, were mentioned almost twice as often as the next appliance, which was a good stove. This last, however, was named so vehemently as a decent stove, a *good* stove, a good stove with oven, that the answers conveyed a world of frustrated overtones. While the washing machine was mentioned oftener, the refrigerator was repeatedly called a "must" all through the answers. Several underlined the word two or three times and then explained what it meant to them in comfort, health, and economy.

This saves time and money in the purchase and preservation of food.

We feel that a refrigerator with a large freezing compartment will save financially as well as be a real help healthwise. We hope to take one back this time.

Excellent kerosene refrigerators and gasoline washers can be obtained at reasonable cost, as well as the more conventional electric and bottled gas models, so most missionary women can avail themselves of these basic helps. It is true that a good washerwoman is a satisfactory substitute for a washer, but she is generally harder on the clothes, especially if she hangs them on cactus or barbed wire or thornbush to dry.

Several mothers spoke of good bottled-gas stoves and how grateful they were for them. Of course, being able to use one of these depends on where one lives. Kerosene and gasoline stoves and gasoline irons are all an improvement over wood heat and flatirons.

Some specified an automatic washer, and said it had been a "wonderful help." No doubt they were in a situation where both water and power were adequate. In the absence of these an automatic washer can become a headache and a frustration rather than a help. Some missionary suppliers do not recommend them for use unless there are facilities available for servicing them. On the other hand, if the conditions are right, an automatic washer can free a missonary as few other appliances do, and a good washer or dryer can be counted on for years of trouble-free service.

In a wet climate a dryer is a delight, especially for a mother of young children who has had to hang out clothes two and three times to get dry. This appliance alone, in proper circumstances, can add up to two hours to a woman's day, and has protected her health to a marked degree. It has one other rather unexpected advantage: it does away with "clothesline thefts" by passersby. In some places a dryer has saved many missionary dollars in this way alone.

The electric mixer was mentioned somewhat oftener than the dryer, and stainless steel bowls were specified to go with it—stainless steel does not break.

Other appliances that were particularly appreciated by some were the sewing machine, the electric steam iron, the pressure cooker (or pressure canner), and the electric blender for mixing powdered milk. These are a continual blessing to those who have them.

This list ends with the women who at one extreme would gladly settle for running water and electricity (one of these was a home missionary working among the Navajos) and the women who were grateful for the use of an electric skillet, floor polisher, vacuum cleaner, and toaster.

As one mother wrote, "Almost any appliance is a blessing." But too many appliances can also become a burden. For her own good, a woman will avoid heaping up to herself appliances or household goods in any overwhelming amount. Somehow possessions in too great abundance have a tendency to stifle and choke, and even to make for separation from the people the missionary has come to reach. If such is the case, a woman does well to meditate earnestly on the verse in which the Lord said, ". . . the care of the world, and the deceitfulness of riches, choke the word, and he becometh unfruitful" (Matt. 13:22). Missionaries are sojourners who want to travel light.

While servants and appliances have the chief function of saving the missionary mother's time and strength, there are certain duties which she herself must attend to. Normally she will supervise the marketing, the planning of meals, the cleaning of the house and, of course, the private care of the children.

The chief problem, then, is how to determine the most efficient use of her household time.

The first step has already been suggested. It is the obtaining of whatever help is available and, in the case of servants, taking initial time for careful training. Another possible source of help is found in a judicious selection of modern materials for use in a house. Today plastics are used for many, many items—from tablecloths to lightweight buckets. Clothing comes in a wide range of wash-and-wear fabrics. Carefully selected, most of these things will move easily from one house to another and will lighten the housekeeping burden appreciably. Often something more expensive, if the money is in hand for it, may prove to be an economy both in time and expense. One mother of a large family reported a saving of three and a half hours of work time per laundering by using fiber glass curtains in her windows ($4.98 a pair) in preference to the 98¢ cotton ones that required such frequent careful work on her part.

But there will always be a certain amount of plain work involved in running a house smoothly, especially if there is little household help. Even to train a servant, a missionary must be a skilled housekeeper herself, able to look well to the ways of her household.

MANAGEMENT OF TIME

Mrs. Welthy Honsinger Fisher, herself a missionary in China for many years, wrote a book for ministers' wives. In her chapter on "Managing Your Household Time" she wrote:

> Each job should be simplified so *that the least possible time and effort are used to complete it.*
>
> "It has been estimated that 25% to 50% of the manual work done in our shops, offices, factories, and homes is unnecessary—that the work might be done in a much better way, producing the same output with less expenditure of energy on the part of the workers." . . .
>
> The ease with which you work partly depends upon the preparation you make. This questioning will help you find lost motions.
>
> As you follow the process of dishwashing, cleaning, bed making, ask yourself, "Is it necessary?" Again ask yourself, "Do I reach too much?"[8]

---

[8]Welthy Honsinger Fisher, *op. cit.*, pp. 78-79.

The second step, then, is thoughtful organization. This remains entirely flexible, but it gives a sense of direction to the workaday hours. A quickly jotted list of duties requiring attention, a numbering according to priority, an estimate of how long the job should take, and a woman's competitive spirit is aroused. Just seeing if she can beat the clock can give her the sense of relaxation she would derive from a game. Then when she finishes a seeming hectic day racing from one call of duty to another, the list is a silent reminder that she *did* accomplish a considerable amount!

Sometimes a woman will become conscious of a nagging worry that is inexplicably sapping her energy. It is wise to stop and ferret it out. Sometimes it is just the way her fellow missionary spoke to her, or her own sense of shame and sorrow at having failed to live Christ before one of the nationals or before her children. Such nagging thoughts can be turned over immediately to the Lord, asking Him for forgiveness or expressing willingness to freely forgive. However, what is bothering the missionary is often something much more simple: a garbage can that needs scrubbing out, a dresser drawer that has been in disorder for weeks, a pile of trousers that has waited six months for mending. It is amazing what emotional relief a woman experiences when she takes time out to do that little thing which has been nagging her conscience. The half hour (or half day) it requires is better than a shot of Vitamin B_{12}.

MAKING MONEY STRETCH

The finances of the household depend somewhat on the missionary's income. It is up to the housewife to make her money stretch. Up to the housewife? There are times when stretching that money is an utter impossibility. At times like that she can relax and watch the Lord God take over. The home in which His glory has thus been manifested is ever after a holy place to a missionary.

The spiritual principles involved are simple. He is "the God who *cannot* lie," and He has said, "Seek ye first the kingdom of God, and all these things shall be added unto you." He has also said, "I will in no wise fail thee, neither will I in any wise forsake thee." Hudson Taylor beautifully expressed this in a letter:

> My need now is great, and urgent: God is greater and more near: and because *He is,* and is *what He is,* all must be, all is, all will be well. Oh, my dear brother, the joy of knowing the *LIVING GOD,* of seeing the *LIVING GOD,* of resting on the *LIVING GOD* in our very special and peculiar circumstances! I am but His agent. He will look after His own honour, provide for His own servants, and supply all our need according to His own riches—you helping by your prayers and work of faith and labor of love. As to whether He will make the widow's oil and meal go a long way, or send her more—it is merely a question of detail; the result is sure. The righteous shall not be forsaken, nor his seed beg their bread. In Christ *all* the promises are yea and amen.[9]

But when there are funds with which to work, the missionary mother can ask just as trustingly for wisdom in the use of them. She must apply herself industriously to the problem, but the Lord will faithfully guide her. The two secrets are wise purchasing of supplies or materials and careful use of them.

If the family is large, quantity buying can be a partial solution. One danger is that in the face of seeming abundance the family will use more of those items than necessary, and then the savings will have vanished. The mother will need to exercise reasonable control of supplies.

COOKING AND ENTERTAINING

She can also learn to cook well the dishes her family enjoys. Then by checking periodically on the cost of individual meals she can learn to gauge how much she can do with a

---

[9]Dr. and Mrs. Howard Taylor, *Hudson Taylor and the China Inland Mission* (London: The China Inland Mission, 1927), p. 259.

given amount of money. The essential ingredients for good cooking given to me by a dear German friend were: "Don't forget to put in lots of love and prayer."

If a mother is new on the mission field, she can get all sorts of cooking ideas and tested recipes (how to substitute the native brown sugar for molasses, or how to roast coffee) from her fellow missionaries. She will thank the Lord for her Tupperware or whatever she has that will hermetically seal in her flour, sugar, and other staples, away from moisture—and insects! She will possibly learn to can anything from meat to preserves. Good cookbooks will yield recipes she can adapt to the new foods of the country. Green mangoes make a marvelous "apple pie," and equally delicious apple butter. Omelet with fried plantains in it is delightful, and there is no jam so exotic as that made by cooking one grated coconut with one grated pineapple and an equal amount of sugar.

Always she will try to have on hand foods which can be prepared quickly for unexpected guests. On the mission field hospitality is a deep joy, and the housewife provides for it with forethought, often hiding away a few special cans with which to crown an impromptu "company dinner."

In some cultures it is desirable to serve all visitors something—a cup of tea, a tiny cup of strong, sweet coffee—when they drop in. Some missionaries in country places keep long stalks of bananas ripening for this purpose.

Learning to cook the native dishes of an adopted land will yield double dividends. Invariably those foods are less expensive than imported American foodstuffs, and therefore help to keep food costs down. But in addition, the appreciative use of native foods is sure to endear a family to the people among whom they work. One of the easiest ways to make a close acquaintance with a woman whom a missionary wants to reach for the Lord is to ask for detailed instructions on how she prepares *hallacas* or her special curry. An instant bond will be formed, which the Lord can use.

The average missionary home (if there can be such a

thing) is probably not to be compared with the average American home. It will conform, in some measure at least, to the architectural style of house in the country itself, and the missionary mother will furnish it as attractively as her skill permits. She will give thought to making that home comfortable and convenient for her family and at the same time inviting and restful to their visitors. This will involve prayerful observation of their culture and of their reactions in her home.

As to the level at which the missionary should try to live, one missionary mother wrote:

> Our country has a small *very* upper class and a large extremely low class. It's hard to live at either level, and so we aim at low middle for ourselves. To love them, understand them, think, feel, and to be able to show it in actions, is more important than having home get-togethers.

Another missionary told of having repainted her old furniture and otherwise freshened her living room when a little neighbor girl, daughter of Christians, came in and sat down. "Oh!" the child exclaimed, "Is heaven going to look like this, do you think?"

The missionary will notice how the nationals keep their houses and how they show hospitality when she visits them, and will find ways in which she can adapt her housekeeping arrangements to set them at ease when they visit. Once again, the basic law is flexibility.

CHILDREN AND HOUSEWORK

As the children grow, it will become necessary to include them in the household arrangements. Since the children are rarely a help, allowing them to help is part of a mother's ministry to them. Tiny children invariably love to help, for it is a child's delight to do something along with his mother or father, and a wise adult encourages this. However, as children get older, the household chores tend to become distasteful, at least for a while. This can become particularly irritating to a busy mother who is racing around trying to accomplish a certain amount of work before time for a children's class or a broadcast. She can choose between just letting the children go and doing the work herself—which is easier—or accepting this as one of the interruptions the Lord permits in her day. Once again the twin laws of flexibility and organization come into play. And the mother will prayerfully continue to demand faithful fulfillment of work. One mother wrote: "If I were doing it over again, I would start training my children from a very early age to help rather than wait. I think I could do more if the children helped more in the home."

Breaking up the job into smaller parts by a series of con-secutive commands helps. So does working along with the child. The mother may have to do the work again herself later, but the Lord will at last bring the day when the child will be "grown up in his youth," faithfully taking on respon-sibility.

It should be understood from the first that the servant, if any, is there to help the *mother,* not to serve the children; and they should never be permitted to "boss" servants or leave their chores for a servant to do. A mother from Brazil wrote:

> It will pay big dividends to take time while the children are small to train them to help in household chores and in taking care of themselves not only for the personal discipline but for the physical help it will be in the future. One of the big dangers on the mission field, where household help is practically a necessity, is to let the children grow up accustomed to being served instead of being independent (in the right sense) and helpful.

Children can reduce an orderly, attractive home to shambles in an unbelievably short time. A tired mother just home from teaching a teacher training class—missionary work!—may sometimes feel that there is no use trying to clean up the clutter that has accumulated during her brief absence. (*Why* do people *always* give little children marbles, puzzles, and toys with a thousand pieces?) Probably Daddy was there the whole time, deep in study, but he never noticed what they were doing to the house. After all, nobody broke an arm!

DEALING WITH DISCOURAGEMENT

When a job looks discouraging, any job at all, a woman does well to encourage herself in the Lord her God, even as David did. It is also good to break up the work into small parts. If the living room needs cleaning, she straightens one corner or clears up the couch. If her kitchen needs attention, she gets all the silver into the dishpan, gathers all the glassware into one spot, and begins to scrub off surface areas. As her sense of accomplishment grows, her spirits rise; and soon a spirit of praise to the Lord fills her heart rather than a grim determination. The important thing is just to *start*. One mother wrote, "Don't procrastinate. A job is lessened by immediate obedience."

Invariably, whatever household testing the missionary mother is going through is being witnessed by one of the nationals or one of the children. His acceptance of the genuineness of Christianity may stand or fall on whether the missionary triumphs in the tests that come to her. She dares not walk otherwise than in constant dependence on the Lord for victory.

A house should always be clean, orderly, and attractive. This is the ideal and should be the normal condition of a missionary's home, both for the sake of the testimony and for the sake of the ideals that she will want to implant in the children growing up in her home. Right at this place is found one of the greatest points of conflict in the mother's daily experience. Some mothers are perfectionists. To such a mother the word has a very different connotation from what the word signifies to a mother with a less demanding, more relaxed temperament. But all mothers suffer frequent compunctions of conscience over the state they have allowed things to get into while they were attending to other duties. It is true that a mother must constantly exercise diligence in this matter of cleanliness and order.

However, when a day's anticipated work is far more than can be crammed into twenty-four hours, the missionary mother has the privilege of entering into what is possibly the most valuable experience her occupation can give to fit her better for missionary work.

She begins by recognizing her helplessness to meet the demands laid upon her. Then she looks away from those demands, and "as the eyes of servants look unto the hand of their master, and as the eyes of a maid unto the hand of her mistress," so she looks unto the Lord her God. He is merciful, and His ways are perfect. He leads His obedient child through the maze of tangled responsibilities with such a sense of His direction and presence that her heart is at rest at the end of the day. If she has done His will, nothing else matters.

There are situations "common to man" which most missionary women face at one time or another. Sometimes a woman has no strength, no vitality, and yet her duties are undiminished. This is often the case after illness. Aside from having a doctor track down the cause of her condition, she can take some very simple steps. For instance, she can spend a few minutes out of every hour lying down, relaxed. These can be golden moments when she occupies them in praise. She can thank the Lord for every task He has enabled her to accomplish, but even more she can praise God that He is the One who upholds all things by the word of His power, who is girded about with might, of whom she can say, "The Lord is my strength and my song" (Ps. 118:14).

These times of weakness are especially helpful for the evaluation of tasks according to importance. It will be found that *order* (books and toys put away, clothes hung up) is more essential than sweeping, and sweeping than dusting. Food is more important than frills. Pillowcases and sheets, slips, bluejeans, don't *have* to be ironed. It is what Mrs. Fisher calls "intelligent neglect."

Most important of all at these times is the conscious step-by-step walk with the Lord. The mother learns then to take just one duty at a time, and finish it in the strength He gives, going from that to the next task as He indicates it. It becomes her experience that "the way of the Lord is strength to the upright" and that "to them that have no might He increaseth [the Spanish says "multiplieth"] strength."

Often a woman will find that the lessons learned in these times of physical weakness are the ones that eventually release her from many household frustrations and set her free for active participation in missionary work even while her children are with her. At any rate, from that time on, she knows the Lord's strength to be her very real sufficiency, and she will rest in it.

For a certain period in a missionary mother's life, she seems to be tied down to a house and to housework. The study of the answers to the questionnaires indicates that there is a decided decrease in time required to run the house as the children grow up and go away to school. As a result several mothers are now putting full time into the work, using an hour or less a day to run their homes, if they have servants. It is surely no exaggeration to say that for the rest of their lives they will be far more efficient, more sympathetic, and more fruitful because of the years of self-discipline they have lived through, and the faithfulness and mercy they have found at the hands of their Lord.

CHAPTER 5

HER MISSIONARY WORK

. . . It is true that children do restrict certain types of missionary activity. The missionary mother, in particular, is not so free to travel, to spend long hours in teaching, etc., as her unmarried sister. There is no getting around it; children do take time and call for a great deal of attention. Also, they need a settled home.

But as we have mentioned before, children do have also a ministry all their own. They open doors and hearts to the gospel, and they attract other children and, through them, their parents. Moreover, the missionary mother is nonetheless a missionary for being a mother. Her ministry may be different from that of the single woman, but it is fully as effective. In fact, what has never failed to amaze me, in more than one field, is the amount of missionary work accomplished by some of our most devoted missionary mothers. Perhaps it is because they have learned to make the most efficient use of their time; perhaps it is because they do without some of the primping and fussing; or perhaps it is just because they are so wholly and unselfishly dedicated both to the family and to the work. At any rate, hats off to them! They put many of the others to shame.[1]

M$_R$. Cook's study of the problem of parenthood, especially motherhood versus missionary work, is sane, sympathetic, and extremely helpful. Mothers will be better missionaries if they read the whole book. In a sense, there is no great need of add-

---

[1]Harold R. Cook, *Missionary Life and Work* (Chicago: Moody Press, 1959), p. 97.

ing to the basic principles he has drawn so clearly from Scripture and from experience. They are:

1. In marrying you have voluntarily assumed certain obligations—the normal obligations of married life.
2. Marriage looks forward to parenthood and its obligations. Parental obligations include love, counsel, comfort, and affectionate interest in the children.
3. The Scripture gives no ground to act otherwise just because one is a missionary; therefore the obligations still hold.

He concludes that there need be no conflict. The missionary wife must simply get the right perspective of her ministry.[2]

Proceeding from these principles to the study of how different mothers manage to do missionary work will surely not be amiss, and such a study will be necessary to make our consideration of the subject complete.

OBLIGATIONS AS A PARENT

The questionnaires would indicate that more "missionary time" is available nowadays than formerly. Comparatively few missionaries teach their own children through the grades any more, as good schools become increasingly available. In some cases the children commute daily to school, or on week ends; in others they come home for the longer vacations only. The result of all this is that while the children are still young the missionary mother has been set "completely free" for missionary work as such for many more hours a week than formerly. A mother of five, the youngest of whom is now six years of age, said:

> I hardly feel like a "normal" mother now. I've "been through it." Just this past September, our youngest went off to school. About one fourth of my time is given to the running of the home now. It used to be three fourths of my time when the children were not in school. I would

---

[2]*Ibid.*, pp. 96-99.

then go down to our girls' school for an hour in the morning and two hours in the afternoon.

Another wrote:

> Our situation has been unique in that during the years when the children were small we had charge of a Bible institute and a large part of my work was done right on the grounds where we lived. Later as the children were in school I had work which kept me busy during their school hours and left me more or less free when they needed me.

The years of a mother's missionary service can be divided into two periods, the first of which gradually merges into the second: In the first, the children limit what she can do; in the second, she has no children and is free again. Most missionary children begin going to school at six to eight years of age. The years in which a missionary mother's outside service might be severely curtailed would fit roughly, then, into a formula like this:

Years of limited service = difference between ages
     of oldest and youngest children plus 6-8 years.

There follows a transitional period in which, at certain times, mothers are still occupied with parental responsibilities. However, by this time the children are older, and they may possibly be starting to contribute to missionary work themselves, voluntarily. Many do, though in simple ways at first. A mother wrote:

> I have felt that since the Lord called me to do missionary work, the job of mother could fit in more or less equally in preference under normal circumstances. If for sickness or other extreme purposes I had to choose between the two, I feel that my first duty would be to my children. As a mother I can't be as active in taking trips as a single girl, but on the other hand our life and the lives of our children make openings that single girls don't have. The people love our children and I'm sure I have made many friends because of them. The children

have been an attraction to other children. One of our deacons, when hearing that the children were due home from school, said, "That's good. We'll have more of a group when they get here as they bring their neighborhood friends."

This is one of the richest portions of a missionary child's heritage. He doesn't wait to go to Bible school or Bible college for training in Christian service. He starts early to help with younger children in vacation Bible schools or Sunday school. He is in classes, but often begins to feel a sense of personal responsibility for the message to reach hearts. It is well that he be impressed early with the fact that the Gospel of Christ is actually "the power of God unto salvation" and that Scripture is to be applied to the believer's life—that it is to change that life. All the time parents are ministering to others, they are ministering also to their own children who are present and who, from a sense of loyalty to their parents, have become peculiarly open to instruction themselves. Then, as they grow, they share more deeply in the work. As one mother wrote: "By sharing our home with our people, and our hopes and desires with the children, they become in a real sense, co-laborers. In their minds the Lord's work comes first."

A missionary mother added to the answers on her questionnaire the following notation:

I can't say by far that I have a normal life, but it is a WONDERFUL one with Him. The Lord also gave me a wonderful husband. Even before the girls became old enough to help here in the Retreat, I always took them (with the exception of one summer) to the children's meetings I had in the mission tent—children's evangelistic campaigns we held. They always enjoyed them and became burdened early for other children. Because of our being a close family, we shared many things with the children, even though they were so little. As time went on, we shared even more, so that now they feel a real part in the ministry. I thank the girls a lot after and while they are helping me. On the other hand, I don't take advantage of them. I let them take as much a part in the activities of the Retreat as possible and only call them if I see I won't be done in time. It is really a wonderful relationship we have and one for which I am *so* thankful.

ATTITUDE OF HER HUSBAND

The amount or type of work a woman can do during her children's early years depends partly upon her husband: his work, his opinions, his willingness to help. His work, because, for example, if he must be away from home most of the time, it naturally follows that the mother will not be free to absent herself from home regularly, leaving the children to their own devices. She will then do her missionary work at home or take the children with her. One such mother wrote:

> In 1958 we went to a new type of work—literature distribution. By this time three of our children were in school most of the time, and we had the two small ones home with us. My husband was away most of the time on school days, often from Monday morning until Friday night, carrying literature to the schools. My job was corresponding with many groups of readers, answering questions, advising groups on organization, etc. This was a very suitable job, as I could spend many hours at it when opportunity arose, but it could also be left for days at a time if pressure of other work made this necessary— such as when the children were home and I had to get their trunks packed for returning to school. I used to figure I averaged about twenty hours of office work using my living room as an office at that time, per week.

The opinions of a woman's husband will influence her work because some men feel it is *their* work that counts. They are right, in a sense, but their wives still need some kind of spiritual outlet in witnessing. (One is within the home, both to the children and to any who come to the home.) One mother wrote with remarkable quietness about this sort of situation:

My case is a bit different from most missionary couples. My husband has always felt his work was first (though he never said it). But I had no assistance or encouragement to do more than keep the family. Actually this is about all a young mother can do anyway. Live and learn! Who can say which is *the way?* God's way may be so different from what heads of missions may teach. The question comes back: Do I as a mother of six merit a place on the field when I actually contribute little? The husband's contribution must determine this in my case.

But many a missionary mother has been able to take a far more active part in missionary work because of the thoughtfulness of her husband, who was able and willing to take over the care and supervision of the children for a time. Some missionary couples deliberately plan their schedules so that they dovetail. Several mothers mentioned such planning appreciatively. One from South America said:

Our children went to Portuguese-speaking schools from the very beginning; therefore there were no problems. We were stationed in the city for our first term. Later on we felt the two younger ones needed more private instruction in English, so I taught them for two and a half years (Calvert Course), which wasn't hard either because my husband helped out with the teaching of our son one day a week while I took the younger girl with me when I taught Bible in the public school, and we studied together between periods. It wasn't a "problem" at all. I loved to have my daughter along because she helped me to make better friends with the children I taught. At home that one day, my husband did necessary book work.

The children and my husband cooperated with me and we worked out schedules that always coincided.

Another from Africa wrote:

When the children were smaller I would say that they were our first responsibility in that we would always try for one of us to be at home with them while the other worked. For instance, when I was working at the dispensary my husband would be home, and when he went to the villages to preach I would be home.

Perhaps if we had not had the children to care for I would have been able to go out to the villages for visitation more often, but my work was mainly the medical work, which took all morning. During most of our years on the field my work has consisted of running the clinic, meeting with Women's Fellowship once a week (one week going to a village to preach and one week meeting in the church for Bible study and prayer), teaching reading and writing to adults several afternoons a week, teaching a Sunday school class. As I said, we tried to have one of us home with the children.

The effectiveness of the ministry of this last mother, a second-generation missionary and a nurse, was greatly increased by her husband's thoughtfulness. The housework was done by houseboys, but the care of the children while young was directly in the hands of the parents. In this way the children are properly cared for while young, they enjoy the care and companionship of both parents, which means so much to the child's development, and both parents share more fully in the missionary ministry. Psychologically this is a good thing for the mother, even though it is not always possible. It was interesting to note the attitude of the mothers whose husbands shared the care and supervision of the children. There was little evidence of the basic "mother versus missionary" strain. Apparently, when it is possible, this is a very satisfactory solution.

Here are representative quotations from the letters of two mothers:

I've found I don't have any rigid policies about missionary work. The conflict between "mother and missionary" has not particularly bothered me because I've never been given a job that required long hours away from home. A good deal of it has been what I arranged on my own. However, for about six years I taught school regularly, one to two hours a day, but we were on a big station where the children had others to play with during that time. When I made long trips by horseback to women's meetings in the churches, my husband was usually able to be home that day, or another missionary would watch our little girl or the older children when they were home on holidays.

Until the time our fourth child was born we lived on a bush station doing medical work (although we are not medical missionaries) and village visitation. Both of us did not usually leave the compound at the same time. Children were often left with a boy while we were at dispensary or other work on the compound within calling distance. Part of the time my husband was also engaged in a good deal of translation work. While he would be on the compound doing this type of work, I would be free for visitation, and when he was trekking, I would work at typing the work already done.

OBLIGATIONS AS A MISSIONARY

It becomes necessary at this point to clarify one more basic relationship. Has it been conclusively settled that one is not only a missionary *mother,* but that she is also a *missionary* mother? *How* can a missionary mother know how much missionary work she is to do, and what kind? For, being a *missionary* mother, she feels a clear indebtedness, a responsibility, to the Lord's work in that place and among those people.

Or does she? There appears to be an increasing tendency among young missionary women in some places to give themselves to their homes and not to the work. One mother states flatly, "I consider my home my ministry." Perhaps, in her circumstances she is right, but older missionaries expressed deep concern about this several times in the questionnaires and letters, and it came out also in at least three interviews with missionaries. Several mothers wrote very plainly. One said:

We have tried to be of help to young mothers arriving on the field recently, for some are arriving with little or no intention of joining in the work, thus missing the "joy" of the mission field.

Another wrote:

I have seen some mothers do nothing in the work. They never mix with the people or allow their children to play or mix. I believe this is a hindrance, and certainly the native people feel this keenly. It depends on whether the wife is a missionary too, *called* also, and her attitude in all this. I think a happy medium for work and children is good—provided no health problems or hindrances come in.

Wrote a mother of five:

More important than how much time we spend with children, and how much time we spend with or in the Lord's work, I believe, is our attitude. Some parents, or mothers, just refuse to do anything outside of the home. It is not what we *DO,* but what we *ARE* on the mission field too. Even though we can only do a little, as in my case, when the children grow up, more and more time is given to mission work outside the home. When mothers come to the field, they are told they must look upon themselves as missionaries (in most mission societies) and help in the Lord's work, therefore, I feel when they come to the field they should not *REFUSE to do anything* once a baby is born but rather seek to be of service in time suitable to them, knowing that as the children grow a little older, more and more time can be given.

The indications in these and various other letters are that this is a consideration that should be carefully thought through before the Lord. Am I a missionary if I do next to nothing in the work? Do I dare occupy myself *only* in the care of my home and family? As one mother wrote:

What bothers me is when mothers on the field have pre-schoolers—have help—cannot do any mission work.

OK *but* also the husband has to spend 50 percent of his
time in the house. What would they do in secular work?

The sense of a personal call to service is so important as a
motivating force; and in the absence of that, there would appear to be a certain spiritual crippling, a stunting of soul, in
the life of a Christian who is content to do nothing at all outside her own home when everywhere about her there are opportunities to make Christ known. The missionary mother
who becomes aware of such an attitude in her own life, should
take time for self-examination and self-judgment.

There is the other extreme, however, and many mothers—
not just young ones—told of having loaded themselves so
heavily with missionary work that their health had broken.
Looking back, they felt they had neglected first responsibilities. One mother told of the reaction on her family life:

> Going to the mission field for the first time in 1959, I
> felt my first obligation was to the work . . . mostly be-
> cause our children had all reached school age, and I felt
> a degree of freedom never before experienced. However,
> I feel that my family was sadly and grossly neglected
> (which is showing its effects now). I feel that often-
> times I gave them responsibilities far beyond their ability
> to accomplish . . . or forced them to be self-reliant
> beyond reason. I do feel that one can shelter her family
> too much (which is often the tendency in a foreign
> country due to diseases and uncleanliness, unfamiliar
> customs, etc.), but I also feel the new missionary can
> go to other extremes, out of a feeling of indebtedness
> to folks at home, as well as the realization of the privilege
> to go. As a result, I wore myself out in the first three
> years, to the place where I was confined for some
> months. . . . I can best explain by quoting an incident:
> At the end of each school day, the children would all
> rush into my room, inquiring as to my state of health.
> At first, when I showed no immediate signs of recovery,
> all was well. Finally, one day when our twelve-year-old
> came rushing in with the question, "How do you feel

today, Mother?" . . . and the answer came back, "Oh, better, I think," . . . There was an immediate look of dejection and the reply, "Ohhh. You do?" It was obvious that she'd rather have me *HOME* and ill, than *At WORK* and well. This was a grave lesson!

WORK LOAD

A husband is often the first to notice that his wife is taking on too heavy a load. One of the blessings of "subjection" to a wise husband can be the protection of a wife's health and her increased efficiency in daily work. Yet most husbands allow considerable latitude in the matter of missionary activity, and a wife must be careful not to inconvenience her husband unduly so that she can feel that *she* is doing "missionary work." As one mother wrote, thinking back over her years of service.

> Concerning the matter of the children and the work, I would "listen" to my husband! The first years on the field I went under the pressure of the field "custom" and took on far more than I could do; and it did none of us any good and the family a great deal of harm. The answer has come for me in being able to fill a *real* need for teaching helps (Sunday school type) in my home. When the boys are gone, I can get out into other activities.

Health is worth watching. A sick missionary must be cared for by others, and her ill health can severely curtail her husband's work. Several mothers mentioned this, and one stated, because of past experience, that she felt she best helped her husband "by staying strong and well enough to carry on the home and look after the family." She continued:

> It is possible to be doing too much work outside the home; thereby allowing the family to suffer. Illness has also been a by-product of too much responsibility outside of the home in former years. It seems I have found the happy medium, but there are always many extras that one does not count on.

ATTITUDES OF OTHER MISSIONARIES

A young missionary also feels the pressure brought to bear upon her by other missionaries, especially her superiors. Such pressure is not necessarily bad. The missionary mother must ever be alert to the insidious danger of becoming involved in home responsibilities to the exclusion of all missionary activity. An effective missionary constantly experiences what is expressed in one letter: "I do not believe the Lord will allow you to decide on a schedule that is within your strength to bear." Whether this was precisely what the writer meant to say or not, it contains a truth worth examining. When the Lord is in command of a life, He makes it far more efficient and productive than we could normally expect it to be, humanly speaking. He gives a mother work to do and then amazes her with the way He strengthens and enables her to do it.

These older missionaries know this and they see the progressive dangers of encouraging inactivity—progressive, because once a mother shuts herself off from outside service, it can become increasingly difficult for her to begin again. As one wrote:

> I think each missionary mother, or any Christian mother for that matter, has to ask God how much outside ministry she should have in the successive phases of her life. For example, when the twins were born, for a period I did nothing but take care of them, run the household, and free my husband entirely for his busy administrative schedule at the time. Other times, I was able to enter into the work a lot. We must wait before the Lord until we have His mind in the matter and then not worry what others say or what others are able to do, but rest in His will. But we must guard against the danger (especially on the mission field I've seen it) of having help with our housework but still somehow not being able to get into the work in spite of having few children. I've found as we look to the Lord for His will, He will give the enabling and strength to fulfill that will and to fulfill the

mountainous task of being mother, teacher, missionary, wife, homemaker, correspondent, etc.

On the other hand, "the poor, insecure young missionary," to quote another letter, "so anxious to please every superior, has a hard time." This mother stated the solution directly:

> I feel very sure that the young mother must seek the Lord's mind as to where her first responsibility lies. To consult other missionaries is not the answer, I feel. It's a case of "condemned if you do, or condemned if you don't." I received it on both scores, because I worked too much outside the home and too little. Once, I really was convinced that before God my husband and children came first, I found inner peace. . . . I should have been more obdurate when posted to classes where the time involved made supervision of the children a recurring strain.

Another mother described this pressure from both points of view, and told how the Lord brought her to a place of rest:

> I think that "older" missionaries make a big mistake and add an unnecessary burden on a young missionary bride or mother when they begin talking about "taking an active part" in the work—that a wife has to be as good (active) a missionary as her husband—that you shouldn't let your children deprive you of doing the work God has called you to do—you must limit the number and size of your family in order to do the work.
>
> Then the "older" proceeds to inform the "younger" of other "inactive" missionary wives. I believe this to be a snare of the devil and a terrible strain on one who is dedicated and conscientious about doing the Lord's work. I find that in our field there is a great deal of criticism towards *seemingly* "inactive" wives.
>
> Up until one year prior to our second furlough I considered myself an "active" missionary wife and was most ready to criticize others (not necessarily by word but by thought) whom I deemed "inactive" for various reasons.

Then I found myself sitting in the others' seat, inactive —and criticized. But I thank the Lord, and say with Psalmist David, "It is a good thing that I have been afflicted." I hope I have learned to be uncritical of others whose lot I do not know and that I'll concern myself with my own faithfulness to my Lord and not with that of others.

I also believe there's a danger of children taking first place, and I think that this too can be overcome and rightful or equal place given to the work with the Lord's help.

To quote one more:

I feel the Lord has a perfect plan for each of us, and our business is not to judge another missionary concerning the amount of time she spends with her family and housework, for He does not lead us all in the same way. However, it is sometimes helpful for an older missionary to thoughtfully and lovingly help a younger missionary find a proper balance. If it is done in the right way, it will be appreciated.

The tendency to criticize one another contributes to the seriousness of this problem. There is great need for humility and for loving sympathy on the part of each individual missionary.

THE SOLUTION

From whichever angle the mothers had faced the problem, the solution was the same. The basic principle is this: that each woman is answerable before the Lord for what *He* wants *her* to do. Beyond this point she has no responsibility. This singleness of mind and heart is the prime requisite for an effective ministry throughout each day. Only in this way will a mother find emotional and spiritual rest before the Lord, the honest sense of having done His will. Once she has this, she need not fear any consequences that may come.

Many mothers have found this secret and rejoice in it. From Central America came this letter:

As to what is "the secret of emotional rest and spiritual quiet in the face of all one should get done and hasn't," obviously the theoretical answer is to rest in the Lord, but how to apply that is sometimes a difficult matter, as you no doubt know. It depends a lot on one's own temperament, I'm sure. But I think that if one can once realize that all that we do that comes to our hands to do, even if it isn't in the schedule and may seem like pure interruption, is part of our missionary service, it does away with a lot of frustration. I try to attack the most urgent need, whether it is practicing with a group for the meeting the next day or mending clothes when the boys just don't have another pair of jeans to wear! And I let the other things fit in where they can. Amazingly enough, everything (except letters!) eventually gets done. Although I'm plagued with the infirmity of lying awake and making plans, and thinking endless hours, it practically never is worrying over all that should have been done, but just wondering how to get everything in. If I don't, well, I figure that it wasn't in the Lord's plan for that day, since He never asks the impossible of us. And I've had to learn that many times our "busyness" is not in His plan at all.

From South America came another:

I realize that the Christian public, mission boards and missions have set down certain rules and standards which are necessary. I also realize that some folks (mothers, shall we say) can get more done than others because of differences in personalities, ability, and health. Circumstances do vary in the different fields also. In each individual case the Lord's guidance and obedience to His will should be sought. There may come our way a lot of criticism and misunderstanding, but, realizing we can't please every man, how wonderful to know we can lean all the harder on the Lord!

And one more:

> I know that I do not have the same problems as some
> mothers who must spend several hours a day in a teach-
> ing or medical work from the home. I realize too
> that I cannot claim to be any shining example of how to
> do two full-time jobs. Many days it seems I have done
> neither of them adequately. But I do believe that if each
> day is committed to the Lord with the earnest desire to
> do His will, He will reveal opportunities for service we
> may have overlooked as well as give peace when home
> duties prevent us from doing all the outside work we
> might like to do. The knowledge that we are in His will
> can relieve the stress we so often allow to mar our joy in
> the Lord and the blessing He wants us to be to others.
> "To obey is better than sacrifice"; and I believe that even
> more than an eight-hour day spent in visitation, teaching,
> or medical work, the Lord wants our loving obedience
> to the Spirit's leading twenty-four hours a day.

The basic principle to guide a missionary mother has now
been stated, and upon it her work must be ordered. She must
find the Lord's will for her personally and obey it.

It has been observed that the time a mother has available
for missionary work is limited temporarily while her children
are young. We will now examine missionary work as done by
missionary mothers, noting first the many different types of
ministries married women have, and then letting different
women tell how the Lord has guided them in combining missionary work with home responsibilities.

DEFINITION OF MISSIONARY WORK

Just what *is* missionary work? Probably few occupations—
except perhaps that of housewife-mother—are so varied; for
missions is the work both of a team and of individuals. This
is why, even when a mission needs a person with specialized
skills for some phase of its ministry, that specialist must be
ready and quick to fit in with other tasks and ministries besides. The work of the missionary woman is in a special way

that of fitting in with and supplementing other missionaries' work—especially that of her husband.

Therefore even the missionary mother herself often finds it hard to distinguish between "missionary" and "non-missionary" work. When asked how many hours a week she could put into missionary work, one mother of six answered:

> I'm afraid I can't put this into hours, for I am often unable to draw the line between what is missionary work and home responsibilities. For example, are the following to be classed as home or missionary responsibility: Preparing and packing food for my husband's trekking trips. Serving refreshments to the evangelists when they come in each month for fellowship and consultations. Preparing and serving refreshments or a meal to those we are trying to be friendly with in order to be a witness to them.
>
> I do teach Sunday School and some reading classes, and do some medical and infant care work (most of the latter being advising and supervising), a little visitation. Yes, I could no doubt do more if I had no children. When I have a class or other work I can often arrange to have it in the house or just outside. If not, my husband or an older child takes care of the small ones.

Another said:

> I have never figured up the hours I put in on the work. Seven months out of the year I have no children at home, and so I'm freer, but, as I mentioned, I don't feel they are a detriment or liability but rather an asset. I feel that the Lord doesn't count our hours in one certain type of work as being for Him, and the rest of the time as not being for Him. Just being at home and receiving the many visitors that come by is service for Him.

The questionnaires, because they represented virtually every type of missionary work, provided a reasonably full answer to those who wonder what missionary women do. The following list presents an interesting cross section of the findings.

There has been no attempt to put the work in logical order, for any one woman may do any five of the different types of work. Missionary women, perforce, are many-skilled and adaptable.

                postal evangelism
                Bible correspondence courses
                Bible institute superintendent of women
                women's classes
                girls refuge work
                playing for meetings
                translation of lessons
                piano and instrumental teaching
                Bible in public schools
                bookstore work
                teaching own children
                speaking engagements
                buying for school or hospital
                art work for magazines
                managing of school kitchen
                running clinics or hospitals
                night-school teaching
                bookkeeping
                hospital kitchen and laundry
                Bible institute wives' classes
                children's classes
                secretarial work
                compound hostess
                scripture and literature ordering and selling
                evangelistic campaign help
                headquarters housekeeping
                writing books and articles
                translation of Scriptures
                children's clubs
                training of singing groups
                MK school teaching
                editorial work
                follow-up work
                correspondence reports for broadcasting

hostess for sick missionaries
counseling
English classes
producing broadcasts, or assisting
nursing—lepers, general nursing
Bible study with individuals
general entertaining
vacation Bible schools
post office for broadcasting station
housemother for missionary children
village work with a Bible woman
handling patients and callers
visitation
sewing classes
radio script-writing
language teaching to missionaries
teacher training
supervising of schools
preparing primers and dictionaries
youth work

Just *how* these mothers do missionary work, especially while their children are young, is a fascinating study in itself. Questionnaires already quoted have given several indications of how it is done. To let a few more mothers speak for themselves, we present more excerpts from questionnaires and letters. These mothers work in every kind of missionary situation, some only a few hours a week and others many hours a day. It should be noticed that, however they are tied down they *have* found ways to serve, and to care for the children too.

A mother of five gave this account of her missionary service as her family grew:

I have found that as my family increased, the Lord graciously lightened the missionary burden. I am a nurse, and I was moved after our third child to a smaller dispensary, and through circumstances after the fourth child, to a station where I was responsible for a dispensary for the girls' middle school—requiring about one hour of work a day—also the missionary children's school, grades one to five (about fifteen children). Also I began to do bookkeeping for my husband's bookstore and became treasurer of our missionaries' children's academy—which work I could do at night. Then after my fifth child I helped at a new dispensary where another nurse was in charge for two or three hours a day. There are many little things one can do to lighten burdens of other missionaries even if it's not in your ordinary line of work. Being at a station where the missionaries' children live, there was a lot of entertaining to be done which all helped with. There is always typing, sewing, etc., little things that one can do in the home.

I would like to be more hospitable and invite more in, but it takes time. While a missionary nurse doesn't have too much of that, I believe it necessary.

Another mother wrote:

This term particularly, since my husband is in administrative work, I do his correspondence. Entertaining is part of our work and just keeping the home tidy and comfortable and things running smoothly is a help . . . I do office work and visitation and have a women's class in my home once a week. I also teach Sunday school this term.

A mother who works in a Bible institute wrote:

I do teaching in the classroom, accompanying the choir, training the women's school trio and sometimes other groups, speaking at the women's prayer meetings, playing and speaking occasionally in other churches or for special evangelistic efforts in the evenings and on Sundays. There are piano lessons for junior and senior women students and several missionary children also. I spend roughly about twelve class hours a week only in teaching in the school. Outside meetings are extra. Yes, I could do more if I had no children, though perhaps not

a great deal more. . . . As a rule, the girls are in school
while I am teaching. The piano lessons are given at
home, so the children are not entirely alone afternoons.
In the evenings when we attend missionary prayer meeting together, sometimes the girls are alone behind locked
doors. Before they were old enough to remain alone, one
of us (usually I) stayed with them, and the other attended prayer meeting. This is what our other missionaries with families also do. We never leave them alone
for any great period of time. Each home has an inter-
com phone, so they can always call if there is an emergency. The school buildings are not far away, with other
missionary homes nearby.

A mother of eight, whose youngest is now thirteen, gave
this resume of her years of missionary service:

When on the field my first term, I taught a literacy
class and visited. I also helped with medical work at various times when needed. My second term I was in charge
of the Mission Home center where many came and went.
My ministry was to "show hospitality" which I found
was a very important part of missionary work. While I
did that I also went visiting in the village nearby and
had a children's class, visited in the town (or city)
among other nationalities than Africans. The next term I
did all the medical work of our station, taught in the
Bible school after the medical work was finished. We also
did evangelistic work, and when we were engaged in that
I took children's meetings and counseled with needy
ones. Took women's meetings also. This we did when we
had no children with us. . . .

I felt I put in as much time in missionary work as
many single workers. I had to budget my time and discipline myself and the children to get it done. As I look
back I feel I did much in the energy of the flesh and I
should have taken some of that time to be quiet and
alone, to be more in the Spirit. I had time in prepartion
for Bible classes but not the time for meditation and
buildup of my own soul. When the children were with us

we left them with an African helper, so we'd be free. I would say six hours of the day were spent in the mission work.

The decision whether to leave children with servants is an individual one. It has been mentioned that second-generation missionaries apparently tend to care for their children themselves, but this has not been proved conclusively. Dr. Soltau says of servants:

> If given the least opportunity, they usually love to take over the responsibility of caring for the little ones, . . . Some missionary parents have quite largely entrusted their women servants with the care of their children, while they have busied themselves with visiting in the homes, conducting Bible and music classes, teaching, and other forms of activity. Others have felt that, much as they would enjoy doing more for the Lord, their first responsibility was the care and training of the children whom the Lord had given to them.[3]

This was further brought out by the answers to the questionnaires. One mother wrote:

> I have never been away from home for long stretches of time. Much of my work has been within sight and sound of the children.

Then another wrote:

> Personally, I could never feel that my children were my sole duty out here on the mission field where I could get a reliable married woman who could care for the children while I went visiting or helped in classes. We had a baby-sitter when the children were small. (She is, incidentally, one of our brightest and most faithful converts from Islam.)

Still another said:

---

[3] T. Stanley Soltau, *Facing the Field* (Grand Rapids: Baker Book House, 1959), p. 102.

While my children were babies, I did "mission work" while they slept. My work then was teaching. As they became a little older, I got a person to look after them for a few hours while I helped out in the school. I never allowed a servant to do for them, however, what a mother should do, such as change them, put them to bed, feed them, or such things.

A fourth wrote:

I think I had one advantage—my children were born there, after I had already learned to trust and have confidence in the native. However, I never had so much confidence that they were tending to either the bathing or diapering of my babes! I find that mothers who have young babes before they come take a long time to acquire any confidence in the Africans.

It is suggested that the practice be followed cautiously.

By far the most important thing to bring out in this chapter, however, is the fact that missionary "work" as such is no impersonal, abstract occupation. The missionary goes out to reach *people,* and to reach them for Christ. Therefore missionary work must always be sensitive to the people involved. Whatever "work" a missionary woman does, she will need to be alert to the spiritual needs of those about her. She doesn't dare become so occupied with duties or so wrapped up in herself and her family that she will not be free to minister to others.

She must never forget this. On the other hand, the Lord, who sent her forth as a laborer in His harvest, is quite able to work in her the love, the tact, the enlargement of heart, the sensitivity to the needs of others, and the skill she needs to touch their lives for Him.

AN OPEN HEART AND AN OPEN HOME

The mother's need for steady, vital contact with the living God has already been considered. Two other qualifications she must have are an open heart and an open home.

Perhaps the first indication of the open heart could be called "availability." A true missionary will not shut herself off from her people. As a wise, loving mother will take time to listen to her children when they want to talk to her, so the missionary will be ready with a sympathetic ear and a wise, prayerful heart when her people want her.

> Whether your work is largely at home or out in the community, one of the hard things is to learn to "do nothing," to make yourself available to others, to be really and wholly present and receptive to whomever it is that needs you. It as hard for Western Christians who come from a culture where activity is so overvalued to regard as *valuable work* the simple act of being wholly present for another. Yet it is often out of just such *work* that deep understanding and trust are established and further significant work is thus made possible. . . . You and your husband may find that you will put less emphasis on efficiency and accomplishing things than you would in most places in North America. You will find yourselves taking more time with people by just being yourselves, at their service.[4]

Then there must be actual communication. This is impossible except as a mother puts forth the effort needed to learn the language. Learning the language is an absolute requirement. A missionary mother must bend every effort to this end, for it is tacit insult to the people of a land to live permanently among them and not strive to master their language. Why should a missionary woman be less proficient than her husband, when women and children will be dependent upon her presentation of Christ to them?

This is a definite ministry. A missionary from Africa wrote:

> Women come to me privately and say, "Oh, I thought if I served my husband day and night to give him his every request, I would go to heaven. Is this not so?" I

[4]*The Missionary Wife, pamphlet,* published by the Student Volunteer Movement for Christian Missions, 257 Fourth Avenue, New York 10, N.Y.

would tell them of Jesus the Saviour, who prepared the way for them, and that only through believing in Him —in His death and resurrection—would they get to Heaven. I explained to them that we are all the same in God's sight—sinners! It does not matter if we are boy or girl, man or woman, white or black. We women are alike before God, for He is our Creator. We have the same number of months for pregnancy and give birth to our children in the same way, and our blood is red like theirs. Some women responded immediately, and others did not.

Over the years the missionary will learn to identify herself with the nationals. It requires adjustment, of course, but it is necessary. A missionary mother wrote:

They feel that with children we're like them—not different like Catholic priests. However our health precautions are hard for them to understand, and we may hurt them by not letting them hold babies—a struggle for me. If I were to live my missionary years over, I'd "worry" less about my home, mix more with nationals, and try to relax more with my family. I've been too frustrated trying to do what I couldn't. I needed first to take care of my relationship to Him and let Him handle the difficulties instead of trying to fight out my problems by myself; for instance my inability to adjust to the ways of nationals (a very primitive tribe).

Another said:

I am learning to pray more over matters, for I have learned more can be gained by waiting on the Lord than by a spur-of-the-moment decision made in haste. The years are also teaching me to "think Jamaican." In the beginning I looked at problems in the light of my background instead of *theirs*. Thinking their way is teaching me to be more patient with their failings and more loving in dealing with them. Also the maturity of years helps us to sense their capacity for learning, instead of expecting too much.

Still another said:

> If we all went out single or as couples without
> children, the nationals would have even further trouble
> identifying themselves with what we teach because we
> would be even more different. Our teaching lived out in
> an actual family situation gives them an example. One
> missionary (among the tribes) said that she got closest to
> the people by doing daily tasks with them such as wash-
> ing clothes by the stream.

The missionary mother will enter deeply into the heart of
her people. She will especially love the women and children
and enter into their problems and joys with a compassion and
sincerity that cannot but endear her to them. As surely as the
people of Naomi became the people of Ruth, the missionary
will find that her very heart is twined around the people to
whom she and her husband minister. There will be a sense of
oneness in Christ between people and missionary that will
make for the "edification of the body" in its practical sense.
Several indicated that times of personal sorrow had drawn
them very close to the people, and had been greatly used of
the Lord.

> We lost a two-year-old with cerebral malaria; he
> took it twice and died the second time. During those days
> of suffering and sorrow, we knew great opportunities
> such as we never would have had otherwise.
> My ministry was greatly heightened by the death of
> my husband on the field. I am now one of the people
> among whom I work. I think unwed women can't get
> close to heart problems of married women.

Isaiah 58:6-12 gives a most striking description of missionary work, worth pondering over. This section of Scripture
reaches its climax in verse 10: "If thou draw out thy soul to
the hungry, and satisfy the afflicted soul . . ."

A book published for missionary candidates has in it the
following passage:

. . . Our doctrine may be sound, our organization perfect, but men and women are hungry for fellowship. Have we found it and can we give it? When we meet together does the presence of Jesus make itself felt,— warm, joyous, strengthening and comforting? Is it easy for us in our church to talk spontaneously of Him whenever we meet? Do we love to listen to the testimonies of one of these 'little ones'? . . . Do we welcome the outsider, and are we able to offer him that which will meet his need in any department of his life? Have we a concern for the brother or sister who is weak or difficult, and can we make them feel wanted?

. . . Can he have true fellowship with the 'natives'? I do not hesitate to say that the majority of missionaries never know their people for lack of this very thing. They go to them with the parental or authoritarian attitude, and the great barriers of nationality, of colour and of mentality shut them out from any possibility of knowing their converts or their fellow-workers in the church. The only place where these barriers can really be broken down is at the Cross, where missionary and 'native' can meet at the same level and get to know one another as sinful men, being redeemed by the One Who died there and rose again. We have got to repent together; we have got to see the Cross together; we have got to be broken together to all pride and self. . . .

. . . But for all those who are willing to pay the price, here is an open door to immense usefulness, and to a human friendship which is inexpressibly precious.[5]

It has been stated that the missionary mother must have an open home in order to reach her people. One missionary was quite burdened about this:

Truly a missionary mother has a very particular ministry—that of "example." But don't we often fail to let the people we came to help get close enough to observe us, so that we fail in this ministry? We are willing to

---

[5]Rowland Hogben, *In Training* (Chicago: Inter-Varsity Press, 1946), pp. 186-89.

make the effort to go *to them,* or teach a class for them in their homes or in the church, but it is difficult to bring mothers and babies into our homes—because of their customs. Oh we did it from time to time, but then I had puddles to mop up and bedbugs in our chairs, and on my whitewashed porch I had many sticky fingermarks after a Christmas party. Part of my trouble was ignorance of their customs when I first got on the field directly following World War II, when we were alone on an outstation because many missionaries were on furlough.

Repeatedly the questionnaires spoke of the joy of missionaries in having homes to which they could invite the nationals, of the enhanced ministry—the reaching of hearts and the opening of hearts to bare their needs—because the people were in the missionary's home.

On the field, it is difficult for the nationals to understand the "single woman" because they have no single women. And so, for us to have a normal home with children helps them to realize we are just like them. Everyone loves children, no matter what their color, and children help to break down barriers and get us into homes and places where we could not have access without them.

Our home provides a place for personal witness to people we could never reach adequately with regular church services. One who is a husband or wife and a parent can present certain teachings about Christian living, duties of wives and parents, etc., with much more force than an unmarried person. For young Christians to see that we also have home responsibilities to occupy our time makes them less apt to excuse themselves as not having time to attend reading classes, to witness, and so on.

Even in the care of the children opportunities will come for witness for the Lord. We found this in our ministry at a bush station. Our oldest child (now thirteen years of age) was the first white child ever seen by the natives of that area, and women flocked from miles around to have a look at her. To all of these groups I was able to speak of Christ—no doubt the first time that many of them had heard of Him.

When we lived in close contact with the nationals they were free to come to our home. Letting our children play with their children was a big help. One of the things that pleased us greatly was the fact that we have had nationals express appreciation for giving our children Spanish names as we had sought to find names that are acceptable in both languages . . ."

We have practically kept open house for our French young people for the past ten years. This has paid off rich dividends!

Nationals will soon know whether they are welcome and free to come to our homes by the attitude we hold toward them. If we are much concerned about our furniture getting ruined, they will soon sense it. In our home we can freely tell them the Gospel, and this is a great advantage, especially if they are apprehensive of relatives.

In chapter 5 it was mentioned that the home of the missionary should be so ordered that the national will be at ease in it. One aspect of homelife which definitely concerns the national is this: What language should be spoken in the home?

It is a difficult question during certain periods of missionary life. When the children have just come back from the States, having forgotten the language of the nationals, it can be irritating to them to have all the conversations going on in a language they cannot understand, and, for the time being, they may be resentful. On the other hand, it is the height of rudeness to speak in front of another person in a foreign language. (Missionaries are often guilty of this fault, even among themselves. The habit must be corrected; it is inexcusable.) As the children learn the language—and, given the opportunity, they will speak it better than their parents—it is well to form an unbreakable rule for the home that when a national is present all conversation shall be in his language. During the period of adjustment while the child is learning the language, the child or the parent should ask pardon if they speak together in English.

A missionary of many years' experience wrote:

> We always felt it was most important to be very careful about how we talked in the hearing of nationals and even among ourselves. If nationals were present we would refrain from speaking English because they could easily imagine that we were saying something derogatory about them. If they heard a name of some worker or missionary they would be sure to imagine we were criticizing that person and perhaps spin a yarn ever so long about things we had never even imagined. A lot of confidence can be destroyed by even one misunderstood word. Be careful about your conversation.

For the sake of the child's future schooling it is well that he learn English and make constant, correct use of it. Therefore he should be taught it on his first furlough, if not before, and English should be the language of the home when no nationals are present.

The ministry of the missionary's home is also a ministry of fellowship. Dr. Soltau has written:

> It is not only important to visit and meet with nationals in their homes but also important to have one's own house and table open to them . . . . While it may be necessary for a missionary to have a higher living standard than the average national, the fact that he is willing to share his home to some extent with a national, as far as entertainment and eating are concerned, will often overcome the barrier made by the difference in living standards.[6]

A mother wrote:

> Tea at any time is a welcome break when our Jamaicans stop by. Over a cup of tea, many problems can be talked over and burdens lightened.There is always a word

⁶T, Stanley Soltau, *op. cit.*, p. 31.

of prayer before they leave us. If they should stop by at prayer time, we simply continue, sharing the blessing of this time with them.

Dr. Eugene A. Nida presented the relationship thus:

The fact that missionaries frequently live in what is nothing less than a mansion, wear clothes incomparably superior to what those around them can afford, and eat not only strange but expensive, imported food might seem to constitute a major obstacle to the missionaries' contact with the people; yet the gulf of material possessions seems to be relatively unimportant unless, as is too often the case, it only symbolizes or reinforces a spiritual separation, often described as "mission compound psychology." There are the relatively rich and the poor in all societies, and people do not hate the rich solely because of their riches, but because of the real or imagined contempt of the rich for the poor. Identification with the people is not attained by wearing a breech-cloth, eating manioc and termites, or dwelling in a grass hut; what really counts is having a mind which can understand, hands which join with others in common tasks, and a heart which responds to others' joys and sorrows.[7]

The son of a missionary submitted an article written by his mother for her mission paper. It is titled *"MISSIONARY-*mother . . . or Missionary-*MOTHER?"* and the article is such an excellent summary of the whole problem that we give it here almost in its entirety.

. . . During our years here the Lord has taught many valuable lessons. One is: God has no standardized pattern for all missionary-mothers. He knows and understands our varying circumstances, abilities, burdens, strength, and hearts. Thus, in infinite wisdom He guides each of us individually into a life of fruitfulness. But the significant question is: Am I letting Him plan, enable

---

[7]Eugene A. Nida, *Customs and Cultures* (New York: Harper & Bros., 1954), p. 257.

and bless while I rest in His faithfulness *OR* am I planning, trying, struggling—and missing His full blessing?

My observation (and experience) is that the enemy would have us follow either of two extremes—his favorite strategy. On the one hand we may decide that God has called us to the ministry of being a good wife and mother—only. Concerned only with our own families, our vision tends to become circumscribed, and we're easily discouraged. Perhaps we even wonder why we've been "put on the shelf" while others push ahead. Inevitably devotional life reaches a low ebb as well. I've discovered that it's easy to use our children as an excuse for neglect of other important things, often deceiving even ourselves and rendering our lives virtually useless while we lull ourselves into thinking we're doing our best.

On the other hand, we may decide that missionary activity comes first—always. We're determined that nothing shall come between us and our service for the Lord. No, not even the needs of our families. But can it possibly be God's will to turn over the training and discipline of our little ones to even the most capable helper with only "spare-time care" from dad and mom? We may discover too late our children are slipping away from the Lord and bringing shame rather than blessing to His name. If we should fail in this paramount task of training our children in His way, how can we expect God to use us in winning and training others? This exaggerated feeling of responsibility toward the Lord's work often leads to frustration instead of the deep, settled peace known only in His perfect will.

Either of these extremes may lead to tragedy. Then which course would the Lord have us to follow? Proverbs 31:26-28 gives us clear teaching concerning our duties as well as a precious promise of a sure response.

Spending much time with our children in their early years may not outwardly seem to be as fruitful as teaching several Bible classes. Yet as we talk with Him daily,

He'll bring from this "hidden ministry" praises to His Name as our children grow to love and serve Him. For many mothers opportunities for an outside ministry may have to wait a few years, but who can measure the value of a life of constant intercession and personal witnessing?

Here are a few practical suggestions:

1. Let's be persistent in training our children in His Word, faithful in discipline, balanced with plenty of love. We must be consistent in our daily example of holy Christian living.

2. Let's not neglect our language study! I'm firmly convinced that we must set aside a definite time for study, whether much or little, or it will be crowded right out of our schedule. Not as easy as it sounds, I know, but with the possibility of many years to serve Him here after our children are grown, how much easier it will be if we can speak fluently and effectively.

3. Let's be untiring in our prayer ministry for our husbands, our children, and all those whose lives we touch.

4. Let's not "bolt the door" against opportunities for service while the children are small, but let's be careful to KNOW He's leading.

5. Let's guard carefully the use of our time, not letting even good things take the place of the best. Unnecessary reading, or too frequent entertaining can subtly rob us of valuable time. Time spent over an ironing board, dishpan, or mending basket can be well used as moments of worship, praise and intercession.

6. Is letter-writing a chore? Let's pray that the Lord may use our pens (or typewriters) as an effective means of challenge and blessing.

7. Above all, let's ask the Lord to live out His love and joy through us so that many a casual conversation may become a vital soulwinning witness for Christ.[8]

---

[8]Eldora J. Schwab, "MISSIONARY-mother . . . or Missionary-MOTHER?" *Japan Harvest*, Vol. 5, No. 4 (Fall, 1957), p. 57.

CHAPTER 6

HER FELLOW MISSIONARIES

ONE ENTERS upon this chapter with a certain reluctance. Why should there be reason for the statement that the problem of missionary relationships is "one of the most critical problems in missions and always has been"?[1] Logically it would appear almost incredible that when the Lord of the harvest has given to all His servants "every spiritual blessing," (Eph. 1:3), granting unto us "all things that pertain unto life and godliness," (II Peter 1:3), missionaries should still be having trouble getting along with one another.

Actual conditions are particularly puzzling then in view of the fact that the Lord Jesus gave one primary command and only one—all the others working out from it—namely, that His disciples love one another. It is a simple strengthening of the command which He said was like unto the "first and great commandment": "Thou shalt love the Lord thy God with *all* thy heart . . ." (Matt. 22:37-38, cf. Deut. 6:5; 10: 12). In other words, the Christian's love for the Lord his God finds its outlet in love for his fellows, his brethren in Christ.

It is no small measure of love which He demanded when He said, "A new commandment I give unto you, That ye love one another, even as I have loved you." Such a love should certainly be sufficient for the exigencies of missionary life . . . one would think.

There is a statement to which some may perhaps take exception, but which women should very seriously examine. It

---

[1]H. R. Cook, *Missionary Life and Work* (Chicago: Moody Press, 1959), p. 117.

is the conviction that missionary women are at the root of the great bulk of missionary personnel problems. While this could perhaps be understood since woman's emotional makeup is what it is, the sweeping provisions and command just considered apply to missionary women as completely as to any other Christians.

What can be done about the problem of missionary women as the cause of many missionary personnel problems?

Perhaps the first constructive move is to acknowledge that the condition exists, and that it is unnecessary. Both of these premises are easily granted, but to apply them to the inner life of a missionary mother will be costly and will hurt.

Mothers are supposed to be grown women, mature and capable of guiding young lives as they develop. In contrast, the Bible says that when the Lord's people are guilty of jealousy and strife, they are immature and are fleshly—not spiritual. The Apostle Paul wrote to the Christians at Corinth, "I . . . could not speak unto you as unto spiritual, but as unto carnal, as unto babes in Christ . . . for whereas there is among you jealousy and strife, are ye not carnal, . ." (I Cor. 3:1-3)? "Now the works of the flesh are manifest, which are . . . enmities, strife, jealousies, wraths, factions, divisions, parties, envyings, . . . and such like," says Paul (Gal. 5:19-20). How can missionary women bring to maturity the babes in Christ entrusted to their care when their lives are marked by strife and friction?

Again the Lord Jesus expressed His desire, in that wonderful prayer of John 17, that believers should *all* be *one,* that the world might believe that God sent Him. He voiced this request twice (vv. 21, 23) as though to emphasize its importance.

It follows that missionary women are sinning against both the church and the world—as well as against the Lord who sent them to win the lost to Himself—when they allow discord and friction among themselves.

The second constructive move must be to acknowledge the utter sinfulness of this carnality and to completely repent and turn from it. A missionary mother dares not grant herself the luxury of self-centeredness. The issues at stake are too important. It's only God's will and His glory that count. Does she really believe her God can work His will and glorify Himself in answer to prayer alone, even if in her opinion everything is being done wrong? Does she really try to obey God's will as expressed in Romans 12:10: "in honor preferring one another"? Does she realize that His command, given through the Apostle Paul in Philippians 3:3, is that she esteem the other better than herself? Does she really love Him? Then why the friction?

The mother finds in her own home—in the actions of her children—a picture of herself as an immature, fleshly missionary.

1. A child wants the best and biggest for himself. This is the sort of thing on which a woman can easily stumble. "Things" mean so much to a woman, and so does the approval—or lack of it—of others. Any imagined neglect can stir up the selfishness out of which jealousy grows, and jealousy stands high in lists of missionary personnel difficulties.

> Of what are missionaries jealous? Lots of things. There is the fellow who seems to get the language so much more easily than you do. Or the one who always seems to have such interesting adventures to tell about. Or the one whose house is so tastefully furnished and his family always so well dressed. There is the missionary to whom the people seem to turn spontaneously for advice, while they pass you by. There are some who seem to have five talents, while at times you wonder if you have even one. There are some whose names appear frequently in the mission publication, while yours is scarcely ever mentioned.
>
> There is plenty to be jealous about if you look for it. And the trouble with jealousy is that it leads to resentment. . . . Yes, jealousy is a real danger in missionary relationships.[2]

---

[2]*Ibid.*, p. 120.

2. A child needs to bolster his self-confidence. This he does by seeking praise or by tattling on another child. An immature missionary will find herself caught up in waves of criticism, which is perhaps the most deadly of the tools the enemy of our souls uses to sow discord among brethren. It is a temptation to criticize, and it may become a habit, and though one may criticize, with no malicious intent, "its effect is still deadly."

> Criticism is a poison. As such it should be used sparingly and with extreme care. . . . We seldom realize just how much our criticism does to embitter our own spirits and poison our lives.[3]

This again is a besetting sin of women, bringing forth the tacit accusation of the Apostle Paul to Timothy as a professional warning between preachers: "And withal they learn also to be idle, going about from house to house; and not only idle, but tattlers also and busybodies, speaking things which they ought not" (I Tim. 5:13).

3. A child dislikes rules. As grown-ups with a taste of liberty, younger missionaries find it hard to submit to older ones. And any missionary may at times find it difficult to abide by rulings laid down by the mission. Sometimes this bothers men more than women, but wives too must be on guard against this attitude and, for the Lord's sake, be submissive to authority.

4. A child hates to be "bossed" by his brothers or sisters. And yet this is one of the basic relationships of the mission field. Someone must be in charge of the station; someone must supervise a general area or project; and in the course of events clashes of opinion are bound to occur between people so strong-minded as missionaries. This is particularly trying when each one is sure he has the mind of the Lord. A woman can add fuel to her husband's fire by dwelling on the unreasonableness of the fellow missionary, or she can join her husband in prayer that the Lord may either set them free to do what

[3]*Ibid.*, p. 125.

they feel He wishes or give them a clearer understanding of His will. In her own field a woman may resent the advice or counsel of another missionary. The Lord has commanded His own to be "clothed with humility" and to be "subject one to another" (I Peter 5:5).

5. A child is slow to adapt his behavior for the comfort and convenience of others. Immature reactions to petty irritations can build up to serious difficulties on the mission field. Mannerisms and habits can annoy fellow missionaries to distraction, and a mature missionary will seek to eliminate any such habits even when they are in themselves harmless. Toward others, she will cultivate a relaxed attitude and an appreciation of the other person which will minimize friction.

6. A child has a fixed point of view—his own. Most misunderstandings that plague a missionary body have their origin in selfish viewpoints which are tenaciously held. A woman must seek to put the best possible construction on what others say or what she hears about them. She must learn to talk over problems with a fellow missionary in friendly fashion so as to clear up misunderstandings. When she cannot do that, she must commit the situation to the Lord, lovingly and without resentment.

7. Finally, a child has poor perspective of time and values. Even the most mature missionary is still in need of walking with God, her heart not haughty nor her eyes lofty, letting Him direct her activities and those of her fellow missionaries, but seeking to understand the ways of eternity, to see things and people as God sees them.

The questionnaires and interviews yielded suggestions from missionaries on what it takes to live in harmony with other missionaries. It was of interest that, of all the questions that might have provoked long discussion, this one received almost uniformly brief answers, packed with meaning. They added up to what should be helpful guideposts to the woman who deeply desires to please the Lord in this matter.

The question asked was: "What do you feel most important

in your relationship with other missionaries?" This is a composite of all the answers:

1. A warm love in my heart for each one. "By this shall all men know that ye are my disciples, if ye have love one to another." A love that overlooks slights— when others receive invitations and you do not. Love from the heart, no matter how different they are from us. Thoughtful consideration of their feelings, desires, work. A real appreciation of their individual worth, of their abilities and accomplishments. True, prayerful interest in their lives.

2. Humility—realizing that the Lord has called them too and they have just as important a part in the work as I do. A willingness to help and to yield; a giving of oneself to them, "in honour preferring one another." One must seek to go the extra mile, to overlook the little things, to put oneself out to be helpful and thoughtful and to maintain fellowship. Ability not to let little irritations assume undue importance. Willingness to forgive; learn to forgive *always*. Learn to take injury and forget it. Remember the devil is always dogging them, too.

3. A taboo against gossip. Consider fellow missionaries as individuals, with differing needs and problems. Avoid a critical spirit. "The law of kindness is on her tongue" (Prov. 31:26).

4. Frankness, honesty, openness. Keep problems in the open. Keep short accounts; settle misunderstandings immediately. If you don't, misunderstandings can so easily build up and become mountains, and a mountain is so much harder to remove than an anthill. "Frankness" is "speaking the truth in love" (Eph. 4:15).

5. "Empathy" or understanding in the sense of putting yourself in the other person's place, trying to feel what he feels in a particular situation. Hospitality; having a bed and food ready whenever fellow missionaries pop in, but especially joyful fellowship. Companionship, contact in informal fellowship. A cordial, friendly rela-

tionship with all, not too thick with any, though some are naturally dearer than others. All missionaries are hungry for plain fellowship. (This doesn't involve telling all your private affairs.) "Owe no man anything, save to love one another" (Rom. 13:8).

6. Take care not to overdo the social aspect. "Don't live in the same patio." "Stay in your own back yard." "Let thy foot be seldom in thy neighbour's house, lest he be weary of thee, and hate thee" (Prov. 25:17).

7. Avoid jealousy, bitterness, clashes based on personal feelings. Be willing to accept correction, and when you offer correction, use tact. "If you have bitter jealousy and faction in your heart, glory not and lie not against the truth" (James 3:14).

8. Sincere respect for superiors and novices both, even when they don't do things as you think they should. Respect for opinions of others, and obedience to rules. "Subjecting yourselves one to another in the fear of Christ" (Eph. 5:21).

9. Share together in the work. Talk over problems and exchange ideas so no one can feel he is left out or lonely. Oneness of purpose without competition. "Doing nothing through faction or through vain glory" (Phil. 2:3).

10. "And certainly prayer together is a MUST." Prayer fellowship and fellowship in the Word. Prayer for common needs and problems, daily or as often as possible. "Supplication for all the saints, and on my behalf, that utterance may be given . . ." (Eph. 6:18-19).

Four mothers gave quite full answers which I quote:

> I think that one shouldn't live too close to other missionaries. In the large town this isn't such a problem. We lived with another couple in the same small town for eight months. I'm glad the Lord changed the situation just when He did. We are still the best of friends. I'm speaking for our countries where there are no compounds. I also feel that each missionary is accountable to the Lord, and we shouldn't expect all of us to do the work in the very same way and methods. If one has to

work closely with another, prayer together will do wonders. The fact that your fellow missionary understands like no one else does and can pray for you with such understanding leads to a wonderful relationship almost closer than that of brother or sister.

This mother worked on a village station:

I've often unconsciously thought of many of these questions as I observed conditions last term. Although we are all women, we are all different and led of the Lord differently. My attitude has been helped much by realizing this fact. Some of our ladies have four children and are unable to do any missionary work, as was the case on our village station. I was one of the two who carried the "missionary work" load with the Pakistani women. I know the others wanted to help, but there is a limit when one lives in a primitive area, and it takes a lot just to live. I find much joy in what the Lord permitted last term. I'm looking forward to a richer ministry this next term with the Lord's help. It may not be such active evangelistic work, but I feel confident the Lord will direct.

This mother works on a "mission compound."

It is important to allow each family individual privacy in their homelife and in the matter of the upbringing of their families. When one lives as closely together on a campus as we do here, it is possible to infringe upon the rights of others without meaning to do so intentionally. It is well to have the best of relationships with each missionary and yet not to intrude. This is most true about the children—a tender spot with each parent. It is also possible to feel one must know everything about the other family's whereabouts, their activities, their friends—not respecting their individual rights and privileges. Only the Lord can help us to find the right balance, offering friendship and encouragement without an overbalance of intrusion.

This mother's husband works with missionaries:

> With my husband as Field Director . . . I found it
> necessary to maintain a free, uncritical spirit toward my
> fellow missionaries. It was also imperative that I not be
> a gossip center, in order to maintain their confidence in
> my husband's ministry. But we all enjoy one of the
> sweetest fellowships I know. This has been welded to-
> gether through a monthly day of prayer, a meeting which
> we all expect to attend. Now, with the number of chil-
> dren ever increasing, we plan a program for them to
> coincide with the adults' hours of prayer and, as moth-
> ers, take half-hour turns at supervising their worship
> and play. I think only united prayer can bind mission-
> aries.

To add a few somewhat unrelated comments to the above:
Missionary mothers could be of great blessing and encouragement to single women who are on the field. There is
a possibility for companionship and fellowship there that can
enrich both lives greatly. Children should be taught to respect
and love these fellow missionaries, and not to impose on them.
There are some missionary homes where the single women
missionaries never feel welcome. The result is broken fellowship, unnecessary heartache, and mutual deprivation. One
mother wrote concerning this:

> Often a wife and mother will have in her home a
> single missionary girl. She needs to ask the Lord for
> great wisdom in making the girl feel a real part of the
> family, yet respecting her privacy. There is need for sin-
> cere love and consideration, for friendliness without
> being obtrusive.

The second observation is well expressed by Dr. Soltau:

> It is a serious mistake for missionaries to discuss each
> other's failings with national Christians. Quite often an
> aggrieved brother or sister will go to one missionary
> with a sharp criticism of another. It is, of course, proper

to listen with courtesy and sympathy and to seek to help in any way possible to make things right. All possible excuses should be suggested as to why the criticized action may have been taken, but under no circumstances should one criticize a fellow missionary, or find fault with another, before a native Christian; nor is it wise, as a rule, to encourage the aggrieved ones to come to you for sympathy unless there is a very real reason. In this latter case, a tactful presentation of the whole matter to the foreign missionary who has caused the hurt may give him an opportunity to put things right.[4]

Finally, when one missionary has sinned against another, there are two possible courses of action, but neither one involves open friction before the church and the world. The name of the Lord is likely to suffer if it does. If frank discussion does not solve the problem, then the missionary who desires the Lord's glory must simply "take wrong" and "be defrauded." The Canaanite and the Perizzite are ever in the land (cf. Genesis 13:7), and she dare not forget it. Earnest, loving prayer for the erring one will heal the hurt, and in time the Lord may even bring that one to repentance. Whether He does or not, the mother is freed to serve on, without hindrance.

The Bible is so practical about this. "If it is possible," it says, "as much as lieth in you, live peaceably with all men" (Romans 12:18).

Perhaps the most humbling experience of all for a woman is to find that she herself is an irritation to a fellow missionary, and to face the fact that there seems to be nothing she can do about it. Given such an opportunity, the Lord will work entirely apart from her weakness and glorify Himself. He takes wave after wave of that daily humiliation and uses it to bring forth the pearl of a life conformed to His image. It's His work, and no one knows that so well as she herself.

It is incredible how much spiritual energy can be dissipated

---

[4]T. Stanley Soltau, *Facing the Field* (Grand Rapids: Baker Book House, 1959), p. 87.

just in trying to get along peaceably on the mission field; but that is the work of the enemy, trying to divert a missionary's attention from her primary reason for being there. The pity of it is that it is all unnecessary. But there is joy in knowing that the Lord has made full provision that the body may be one, each part edifying the whole, in love. The daily application of I Corinthians 13 will enable Christians to live together in such fashion that the world will know that God sent Christ (John 17:23).

The direct application of Scripture will solve personnel problems. The only need is for the personnel to simply obey such commands as:

> Put on therefore, as God's elect, holy and beloved, a
> heart of compassion,
> > kindness,
> > > lowliness,
> > > > meekness,
> > > > > longsuffering;
> forbearing one another, and forgiving each other,
> > if any man have a complaint against any;
> > even as the Lord forgave you, so also do ye:
> And above all these things put on love, which is the
> > bond of perfectness.
> And let the peace of Christ rule in your hearts, to
> > the which also ye were called in one
> > > body" (Col. 3:12-15).
> Who art thou that judgest the servant of another
> > (Rom. 14:4)?

The Lord enable missionary women to love in deed and in truth, and to find in their fellow missionaries the mutual strength and joy that He intended. For,

> . . . working shoulder to shoulder for the Lord in
> mutual trust and confidence, a bond of love and affection
> is built up which grows deeper and stronger with the
> passing of years and proves to be a stimulus to faith
> and a source of courage and strength to all concerned.[5]

---

[5]*Ibid.*

CHAPTER 7

HER HOME CHURCH

Since the days when the Holy Spirit told the church at Antioch to set apart Saul and Barnabas for the work whereunto He had called them, missionaries have, almost without exception, represented some group of believers somewhere. It is necessary to consider briefly just what this relationship entails for the missionary mother.

It goes without saying that a woman's first responsibility to the home church (which here represents her praying and giving constituency) is a faithful fulfillment of her missionary duties. However, beyond this point she has two primary relationships with her home church while she is on the field, and these in turn produce two responsibilities.

The first is a prayer fellowship. The missionary often recognizes that the reason the Lord has been able to bless on the field has been due directly to faithful intercession. Apart from the presence of the Lord Himself, this is the missionary's most precious, most prized help—one without which the missionary would be perhaps of little use.

While true intercessors will pray on faithfully, with a holy imagination (subject to the Spirit of God) guiding their prayers, it follows that there should be a definite effort on the part of the missionary to supply facts, needs, problems, prayer material, to those in the homeland who are willing to pray.

MISSIONARY NEWS LETTERS

A thoughtful study of the letters of great missionaries of other years gives wonderfully stimulating patterns for the kind of letter-writing involved in this prayer fellowship. In an earlier chapter reference was made to the prayer habits of James O. Fraser of the China Inland Mission. Equally outstanding was the prayer fellowship he maintained through faithful correspondence with the several prayer circles that cooperated with him in constantly upholding the Lisu people before the Lord. One of his letters (full of detailed explanations, descriptions, and narrative, as his letters to them always were) expressed clearly the three-way relationship between the home prayer circles and the Lisu and Kachin people, and his own responsibility to them both as he saw it.

> They would be easily able to support their own pastors, teachers and evangelists . . . and it is *fitting* [that they should] . . . but spiritually they are babes, and as dependent upon us as a child upon its mother. They are dependent on us out here for instruction, guidance, organization; but they are dependent on the home churches in England and America in a deeper sense, for spiritual life and power. I really believe that if every particle of prayer put up by the home churches on behalf of the infant churches of the mission field were removed, the latter would be swamped by an incoming flood of the powers of darkness. . . . This seems actually to have happened in church history. . . . Just as a plant may die for lack of watering, so may a genuine work of God die and rot for lack of prayer.
>
> Why prayer is so indispensable we cannot just say, but we had better recognize the fact even if we cannot explain it. Do you believe that the Church of God would be alive today but for the high-priestly intercession of the Lord Jesus Christ on the throne?
>
> . . . You will see from what I am saying that I am not asking you just to give "help" in prayer as a sort of sideline but I am trying to roll the *main responsibility* of this prayer warfare on you. I want you to take the BURDEN of these people upon your shoulders. I want you to

wrestle with God for them. I do not want so much to be a regimental commander in this matter as an intelligence officer: I shall feel more and more that a big responsibility rests upon me to keep you well informed . . . Anything must be done rather than let this prayer-service be dropped or even allowed to stagnate. . . . All I want to do is, as a kind of middleman, to bring the supply (God's grace to meet their need) and the demand (the lost state of the Lisu and Kachin) together.[1]

The number of letters written by great missionaries such as Hudson Taylor, Charles Cowman, William Carey—and the quality of the letters—cause one to marvel. These men, without typewriters or mimeographs, wrote constantly and challengingly, in all sorts of situations, and their letters were faithfully blessed of the Lord to stimulate prayer. Not only did they find time to write, but their wives also found time to write. Indeed, most missionary letters nowadays are written by the wives, as this is one way in which a woman can save her husband hours of time.

In the great rush to accomplish, missionaries sometimes feel that they would rather *do* missionary work than *write* about it. They seem to forget that they are but a link in the chain of God's working. How shall the home church pray except the missionary tell them his requests?

Dr. Soltau recognized the pressure of duties, but he wrote:

The maintaining of the right relationship of a foreign missionary to his home constituency is an important matter. It is too often lost sight of in the pressure of work and the ever increasing demands on the time of every missionary who is "getting into the work" and taking an active part in the numerous church and mission activities. Such work is time-consuming as well as of great importance.[2]

---

[1]Mrs. Howard Taylor, *Hudson Taylor and the China Inland Mission* (London: The China Inland Mission, 1927), pp. 189-91.
[2]T. Stanley Soltau, *Facing the Field* (Grand Rapids: Baker Book House, 1959), p. 93.

Elsewhere is written:

> A missionary has a twofold ministry; on the field and at home. On the field he is ministering directly to the people to whom he is sent. At home he ministers to the church that sent him through the devoted example he sets and the inspiration of the reports that he gives in one way or another. Sometimes the ministry to the home church may turn out to be as important as that on the field.[3]

The second relationship of the missionary with the home constituency is that of giving and receiving. It only stands to reason that if the home group have cared to give and send, the missionary must take time to express his appreciation promptly. Probably there is little question but that these last letters of thanks should be personally, individually written, and that they should also contain prayer material, for people interested enough to give are almost sure to pray. But if every letter received were to be answered personally, fully, and immediately, the missionary would find her missionary activity greatly curtailed.

The problem then, is how to handle a large correspondence efficiently, and yet in a way that retains the personal touch.

The mimeographed or printed missionary news letter has become simultaneously the frustration and the great blessing of the missionary. Skillfully planned, neatly printed, not too long (one page, not too full, is best), and interestingly written, the letter will be—as one missionary mother put it—"kindly received by our understanding constituency." The secret of writing such a letter is that it must be *personal,* both in content and in approach. The style should be conversational. One need not fear the occasional use of the personal pronouns "I" and "we" in a letter, but use them as they would be used in correspondence with one's own family. Such a letter, to which a brief personal note is added, is often a satisfactory

---

[3]Harold R. Cook, *Missionary Life and Work* (Chicago: Moody Press, 1959), p. 137.

substitute for the personal letter one would like to write. Dr. Soltau has said:

> The more the home constituency is enabled to picture their missionary in his home life and daily activity, the more earnest and definite will be their praying and the greater their desire to give of their means to the Lord for the extension of His kingdom . . . Specific requests for prayer, together with grateful reports of the way in which those prayers have been answered, can be a real inspiration to those at home.[4]

When one considers that the great bulk of missionary correspondence is handled by the mother of a family, it is interesting to find that this matter was almost unanimously voted a problem in the questionnaires, and several mothers requested that any help that the study might uncover should be relayed to them. One mother wrote:

> I should think that the best way to tackle it is by writing a few letters each day in a desperate attempt to keep current. I am chronically behind—sometimes as much as six months!

A very few women had husbands who wrote most of the letters, and one wife suggested marrying such a man as the perfect solution! Another wrote whimsically, "I say, the last enemy to be destroyed is *CORRESPONDENCE!*" Of course the mother was right who wrote: "Answer as fast as it comes in. I feel it is the *only* solution and makes for better letters and closer ties." Still, it is not just that simple.

The great difficulty seems to be to find the time for letter-writing of any kind. Several lose a full week of "spare" time when they send out a circular letter, and still don't feel that they keep up properly with what they should write.

It is not that the missionary dislikes the task of writing letters. That may enter in subconsciously, of course. It is that

---

[4]T. Stanley Soltau, *op. cit.*, pp. 94-95.

the correspondence piles up so fast that she becomes hopelessly frustrated. Many mothers feel they do not have time they can conscientiously spend on more than a minimum amount of letter-writing, especially during certain periods. One mother wrote:

> Letter-writing has become a neglected item. It is just impossible to keep a Retreat moving and the correspondence as well.

To look at the problem realistically, letter-writing takes time. A letter would hardly require less than one half to three quarters of an hour to write; most people would need more time from the first quick look at the letter to be answered till the affixing of the stamp on the addressed envelope. One letter would take as long as to prepare for a Bible class, to iron three or four shirts, or to prepare a simple meal (for a mother of only average housekeeping ability). Ten letters a week would take the equivalent of a whole afternoon, which is a luxury many mothers do not have available without interruptions. Then if a mother begins to write after bedtime (and it is a solution some use), fatigue will eventually tell on her nervous system and in her behaviour. There doesn't seem to be any answer beyond what one mother called "sheer doggedness" and intelligent practice in letter writing.

The practice of most families is to supplement what personal letters they can write with a combination letter (the first part mimeographed, the last part written personally and adding to the general news anything of a private nature) or with an ordinary circular letter to which they add brief personal notes. To close relatives or friends, many write carbon-copied personal letters, rotating the "good" copy through the group.

But several mothers did tell of partial solutions that they had found helpful, over and above these. One time-saver was suggested by a mother of four:

> Buy and use a typewriter! Typing is essential for any

missionary. Why waste the Lord's time writing out all letters!

Another wrote:

> This *is* a *big* problem. We often acknowledge letters with a quickie picture postcard.

Several women go over the whole list of letters with their husbands, who generally write the business letters or any of an officially representative nature, deciding on priorities or on the content of different letters. Occasionally a woman will write business letters for her husband's signature, acting as a secretary to him.

One common solution to the problem is, now and then, to give high priority to letter-writing, "as the second, third, fourth, and so on, always seem to come much faster than the first."

Some mothers set apart a certain afternoon or evening each week for the express purpose of letter-writing. One mother keeps a letter in her typewriter at all times, always starting another immediately upon finishing the first. Another told of the following very ingenious arrangement for sending out their prayer letter:

> My husband prints the letters at this end and they are mailed to someone who takes care of the addressing from the home end. While the parcel with the letters is traveling home slow mail, on air-mail paper I write the answer to my letters (some shorter, some longer) and sign them personally. The name is lightly written in pencil (to be erased before mailing) and the letter is enclosed by our correspondent in the correct envelope. Many airmail enclosures are thus written while the letters themselves are traveling home by boat. It gives me about a three-week deadline. My correspondent and I usually arrange a date on which the letters will be mailed from her end, a date when she knows nothing more will arrive for her to enclose.

Several said they try to write a few letters every evening, and others suggested keeping track of incoming and outgoing letters with file cards, marking dates received and answered. One mother wrote:

> One thing that has been a great help to me with correspondence is to keep a little notebook in which I list letters written and the date, with some such note as "pic.," if I've included pictures. Years ago I gave up keeping copies of all letters, for that meant too much of a headache when moving time came. The notebook is such a help in glancing back quickly to see how long it has been since I wrote to certain friends and loved ones —quite a shock sometimes!

Some families, on their file cards, keep pertinent facts about those who write to them: the names or ages of their children, the occupation of the husband, the particular prayer burden being shared with that one. This is especially helpful when the correspondent is someone whom the missionary knows only slightly or perhaps has not met at all.

A missionary who writes hundreds of personal letters a year suggested half-size stationery, and a prewritten paragraph presenting some recent happening in the work, this last to be incorporated into each note, along with the greetings or remarks that make the note personal.

In summary, here are two others. One mother from South America wrote:

> I "keep up" with correspondence, but just barely. For me to solve this problem, it would just be a matter of discipline. Writing letters is, somehow or other, difficult for me, I think, because I have difficulty saying what I mean. Setting aside a regular time for correspondence would be a solution, I think.

This mother from Africa said:

> When something happens worth writing about, I make

a note of it to remind me later. The answer, to me, seems to be in attitude. This is not an "extra," it is *part* of my work. People at home are on the "team" *with us,* and *should* hear from us.

Two final considerations should ease the situation appreciably for a missionary mother. First, letters to the homeland are a necessary part of a missionary's responsibility and therefore are a valid reason for neglecting other work temporarily. Next, a mother can learn to write brief, interesting, friendly letters, and she can discipline herself to do it systematically.

FURLOUGH

There is a third relationship between the missionary and the constituency: furlough. This is an aspect of missionary life which requires special grace, particularly for the missionary mother. Furlough means the uprooting of the parents from their work and the children from their ordered life, and an abrupt transplanting to entirely new circumstances. For a year the whole family lives an unsettled life, and the sense of uncertainty and change has its unavoidable influence on the children, who are in a new (not necessarily better) culture.

The new environment is so different. There is so much to learn—and so much to unlearn! For instance, a four-year-old was receiving careful instruction on the art of toilet-flushing. Her immediate reaction was, "Why? Can they waste water here?" Another little girl, having enjoyed her first ice cream cone, was next taught to sip milk through a straw. Uncertainly she turned to her brother, asking, "Do they . . . eat the straw too?" And a missionary who had recently arrived in the States on furlough wrote back to the field, "The kids didn't take too long to get past the stage where they thought it extravagant to take a bath in the drinking water."

Fortunately, children are very flexible little people. Still parents must make a special effort to help their children to make the adjustment smoothly and happily. Furlough, with its wide travel, affords marvelous opportunities to enlarge a child's horizons. Wise families go out of their way if necessary to see famous places and visit national parks and shrines. Some missionary families enjoy national and state park camping facilities as they travel, and the closeness of whole days and hours in close fellowship as a family can become happy memories that all carry with them in the coming years of separation.

A missionary daughter sounded a warning to parents, however, in the following words about furlough:

> Too often parents—probably inadvertently—give their children a sort of utopian concept of the United States. It becomes, in the MK's mind, a veritable heaven, where he gets new clothes and new toys, where he is "appreciated" and where he is the center of attention. (Every MK knows the uncomfortably delicious feeling that comes as the women of the Missionary Society purr about "the poor little darling . . . underprivileged . . . victim of the Lord's work . . .") This can lead to a "poor little me" attitude when the MK is back on the field. Suddenly he is no longer in the spotlight, and it is easy to convince himself that he *is* heroic and self-sacrificing.
>
> Largely because of my parents' attitude, we kids always looked forward to going home to Venezuela in a way we never anticipated furlough. They taught us through their example that we are happiest when we are where the Lord wants us, and that furlough was just a temporary change—in the Lord's will, of course— largely to give us a quickened desire to get back home.

However, several mothers stated in their questionnaires that furlough was the hardest time of all for them. This seems to be particularly so when the family must do a great deal of moving about, when the father must be away much of the time, and when the family must stay with relatives or friends.

The strain of furlough seems heaviest in this last situation. Normally, such an arrangement should be avoided on any but the most temporary basis. One mother wrote:

One of the greatest problems missionaries have on furlough is housing. Usually their family has increased in number during the years they have been on the field, and although the grandparents are eagerly looking forward to seeing the new offspring, they are usually not prepared mentally, physically, nor financially, to have the tribe descend on them for a prolonged stay. If the missionaries are planning to return to the field, it is most impractical to buy furniture and other household necessities for a short period of use. It is not only impractical —it is usually a financial impossibility. Rent for a furnished house or apartment is also exorbitantly high— and often beyond reach.

Sometimes churches provide living quarters for the missionaries they support. What a blessing this is! Other missionaries are supported by a number of churches, each one having a relatively small part of the support, and therefore not feeling particularly responsible for the care of the missionary during furlough.

I still don't know what the answer is but I feel the missionary mother (and father) will have to face the fact that a settled "home" for the furlough year is a necessity, for the sake of the children's schooling, family relationships, and physical and spiritual well-being.

After living with others for a while, the missionary mother comes to feel that no matter how small or how inconvenient a house or apartment might be, she would rather be established with her family in their own quarters.

Living with others presents so many problems, among them the problem of having a daily quiet time. One mother wrote about her quiet time: "Another frustrating problem, on the field and here on furlough." This is not to be wondered at when a family is on the move or housed temporarily in the guest room of a friend's home. Yet she *must* have her quiet time.

There appears to be only one solution. She will quietly have her time with the Lord off in the bedroom or some relatively calm corner of the house, and let life go on about her. There need be no "holy ostentation" but just matter-of-fact obedience to the laws of spiritual life. The children can be taught to move quietly in a bedroom where their mother or their parents are praying, and not to interrupt unnecessarily.

It is difficult to discipline children under these conditions. At the same time a mother is, or should be on the alert (Christians who have housed missionaries say that some of them are not!) against any abuse or damage her children might cause. For the good name of the Gospel and of the missionary cause, she should replace or otherwise make restitution for things her children break or spoil. It is at this point that a mother is going to reap the fruit of the training—or lack of it—she has given her children.

But even the best-behaved child will find the strain telling on him if his family must live with others for very long. A missionary family is always grateful for a place which they can call their own for the furlough months. Some find it practical to buy a home, when there is a capable friend or church which will keep it rented and cared for while they are on the field. One of the greatest services the home church renders to a missionary is finding a place for the family to live and furnishing it, and letting them use it as they would a home of their own.

Of course, the missionary mother should feel it is her responsibility to see that this home is kept clean and neat and to see that the children use it appreciatively and carefully. This should be the rule whether the church or the missionary is paying the rent.

ATTITUDES

It is of utmost importance that the missionary mother on furlough cultivate certain attitudes.

First would come appreciation, genuine and deep, for anything and everything that is done for her family. This completely rules out complaining about inconveniences or lacks.

Furlough is often an excellent proving ground for the simultaneous experience of the extremes mentioned in Philippians 4:12, "I know how to be abased, and I know also how to abound: in everything and in all things have I learned the secret both to be filled and to be hungry, both to abound and to be in want." It is well known that children absorb attitudes from their parents. It would be difficult to teach one's children any rule of life more important than that of accepting joyously, as a portion from the Lord, all that He sends, with giving of thanks both to Him and to His people.

Second is independence, in the sense that the missionary must never fix her expectation for help of any kind on her constituency. Such an expectation would make her relationship with the Lord's people artificial, for she would be setting her mind on *things,* not on love of the brethren nor on the building up of the church. We read in Hebrews 13:5, "Be ye free from the love of money; content with such things as ye have: for himself hath said, I will in no wise fail thee" and in I Timothy 6:6, "Godliness with contentment is great gain." A mother must permit the Lord to deal with her regarding the sins of covetousness and discontent, that she may serve the church in the homeland with singleness of heart.

The third attitude is her attitude toward service. The missionary family will take every opportunity to fit into the framework of the church, to contribute to its stability and spiritual progress, to stimulate its missionary interest and outreach, and especially its prayer ministry.

Concerning furlough and the many speaking engagements that the missionary fills, Charles E. Cowman wrote from China to a missionary friend:

> . . . When wife and I were on our first furlough, people looked upon us with pity, . . . Some came to our meetings as if they were coming to a funeral. Now why should a missionary meeting be a gloomy one? Tell the people of the victories we are seeing out here, give them the glory side and exalt Jesus. Tell them of the glorious answers

to prayer and don't allow your meetings to be somber and melancholy. Tell the people that we who are "scattered far off among the heathen" are in a winning battle. Tell them we never expect to lower the banner which has been placed in our hands, and as the years pass along, we constantly expect to see the stronghold of sin and Satan beaten down and temples of righteousness rise up on our right hand and on our left, for we "plow in hope." May the Lord use you and your beloved companion in lifting up the drooping missionary banners.

You will find much to sadden your hearts for many of God's children are settled down, "rich and increased in goods and needing nothing." May the Holy Spirit aid you in shaking them up. Keep a warm heart, with God's blessings upon you. We shall look for you home again. Remember that home is out here.[5]

That was sterling counsel, and it is still pertinent for missionaries of this day as they serve their churches during furlough.

[5]Lettie B. Cowman, *Charles E. Cowman, Missionary-Warrior* (Los Angeles: The Oriental Missionary Society, 1928), p. 295.

CHAPTER 8

MATURE REFLECTIONS

Furlough is to be a time of growth. It is expected to be a time of spiritual refreshing through hours of rich Bible study and earnest prayer. A missionary looks forward to the joy of fellowship with many of the Lord's people. As the missionary mother tells of what God has done in her land, she must also deepen in her personal experience of the character and greatness of God.

But furlough is necessary to a missionary from another point of view which missions recognize clearly. Furlough, because of the fact that it removes the missionary temporarily from the scene of her labors, enables her to look objectively at her time of service. It provides the opportunity for an undistorted evaluation of the past years on the field, that she may see in perspective her mistakes, the areas in her life that needed strengthening, the ways in which the Lord was hindered by her ignorance or waywardness. This is to be dwelt on not morbidly but courageously, before the Lord, with the sole aim of correction, under His direction and by His grace, in those areas.

It seemed that a retrospective evaluation of their missionary years by all these mothers would surely be of benefit in this study; therefore the questionnaire included the following questions:

> If you were to live over your missionary years so far, what would you do differently in these matters?

182

This chapter will contain these answers. They provide what is, perhaps, the most intimate look into a missionary mother's heart afforded by the study. Sober and practical, they spoke of heartache and struggle but also of victory. These were items listed:

I would want more time with the Lord. I would set aside more time for daily prayer. I would make more of prayer warfare against the Satanic forces lurking behind the nationals as well as our own children (II Cor. 10:4-5).

More time in prayer for the children, more time in private prayer with each one, and much more time in making sure they learned more Scripture from memory.

More time with the children, better use of the time spent with them. Discipline them better. Have more children. Start training my children from an early age to help. Not overload so heavily outside the home while the children are small. Rather do things that can be done in the home. Not "take it out" on my family.

I would have kept the children on the field even if it meant teaching them ourselves. The work could have been carried on just the same.

I would keep more to a definite schedule; not procrastinate; finish one household job before beginning another.

I would take better care of health; retire and rise earlier; try to regulate my work to line up more with my physical limitations.

I would have refrained from beginning medical work when there were babies in the home—most frustrating. However, I *was* doing medical work one and a half years before the family started. Answer to that? (This was written by two mothers.)

I would keep more closely in contact with the folks at home through letter-writing.

I would take a good Christian psychology course, including study of man's temperament and counseling.

Learn the language better.

Try to understand the nationals better; trust and love

them more. I'd ask the Lord for more patience and a gracious spirit with them. Take them in a little closer; have more of them in the home for meals.

Spend more time with the Christians. Try and enter more fully into their problems and be more genuinely concerned about them.

Be honest with fellow workers and Christians, and the unsaved.

I would be more patient. I would daily seek the Lord to keep me from ever losing my temper. Be less sensitive; not hurt easily.

I would guard my tongue more, and not be led out in criticism nor offer it. Much, much more love for the fellow missionary. I would talk less and pray more. Try not to be selfish with my time.

I would be more kind, considerate, and helpful to the new missionary with so many adjustments.

I would let my husband make the decisions, and provide healthful food and a calm household. I would find more time for missionary work during the years when I had children.

I would go out to the field realizing I know *nothing* about how the work should be done. Thus I would be cast more on the Lord and the advice of others.

I would concentrate more on children's and young people's work; teach adults more of the Christian life; do more personal work.

I would be slower to lead a soul to Christ that showed little evidence of conviction and concern for his soul. I would wait till God did a deeper work in his heart so that once they came they would stand.

All these answers were given in an honest, quiet humility, and the sense of consecration and genuineness was intense. Several recognized strain and frustration as unnecessary, and many spoke of the Lord's goodness and forgiveness. One said:

If I were to live over my missionary years, I would be a far less frustrated mother than I was at first, taking children and opportunities as they come. My motto now is a seeming paradox, "Godliness with contentment is great gain . . . Whatsoever thy hand findeth to do, do it with thy might."

Another wrote:

I would try to avoid useless fretting and work toward a greater trust in the sovereignty of God.

Still another wrote:

I would have wanted more of the Holy Spirit's control. I seem to have learned this so slowly. But it does solve *all* problems.

And a fourth added:

As far as living over our missionary years, I don't know that I would make any fewer mistakes. I'd probably make others and worse ones, being what I am. Our mistakes and sins we have to confess, then forget, even as God does. There's no use wishing we could have done differently. We could land ourselves in a real "slough of despond" if we're not careful. We can always profit by our mistakes in the future, but I generally find myself making others.

Thinking of our failures and omissions, all we can do is rest in His grace and love. Psalms 103:10-14 is a real comfort in times like these. "He knoweth our [my] frame; he remembereth that we [I] are dust." He knows, and in spite of all He knows, He still loves and cares. His marvelous grace exceeds all our miserable failures.

One other impression stood out in all these answers. Along with the recognition of failure and forgiveness was the unmistakable sense of having done conscientiously before the Lord, to the best of their ability, what they felt He had wanted them to do. There seemed to be no boasting or pride at all but only a recognition of facts as they had been. One mother spoke for many when she answered simply, "I honestly do not know."

CHAPTER 9

HER MINISTRY IN PERSPECTIVE

I'm sure you have faced many times when it was hard to decide what should have first consideration, the Lord's work or the children. Enjoy the children while they are small and you have them around you. The time when the missionary family begins to break up is the hardest thing in a missionary mother's life. . . .

My nine living children are scattered far and wide. . . . We have never had them all together since the first one left the nest. But we shall all be together in eternity. . . .

Please leave out my name. You know where I worked. I made plenty of mistakes, but the Lord has forgiven, I am sure.

Your youngest is four years old, mine is nearly forty and is the mother of five lovely children. But don't think I regret that I was a missionary mother and often felt I had to choose between my children and some phase of the work. Not at all; and my children are all happy in the sphere the Lord has placed them in, even if I am lonely at times.

Love to you all.

Yours with prayer,

(Signed by an aged missionary, a pioneer.)

THIS STUDY has dwelt at some length on the problems of missionary motherhood. It is only right that these problems be put into proper perspective and be seen to be what they actually are: a perfect opportunity for the living God to prove Himself sufficient.

As for the unexpected benefits of a mother's missionary calling, they definitely outweigh any apparent "hardship" or "sacrifice," and a missionary mother's life is deeply, wholly, richly rewarding.

The spiritual joys of fellowship between a Christian woman and her Lord are perhaps more keenly savored by the missionary—because of her great need and her helplessness—than by many other Christians.

Missionary couples often endure a great deal of separation. Still there is a closeness, a unity of purpose, a community of interest, that only a comparatively few couples enjoy in the homeland. A missionary husband and wife work shoulder to shoulder, and heart to heart with the Lord.

The children of a missionary have the opportunity to appreciate at least two cultures. They learn to adjust to many situations, and to make friends with ease. As a rule, their education is definitely superior. They have the cultural benefit of wide travel, and their parents can easily take advantage of a travel situation to make history, geography, and sciences meaningful. Usually these children know at least two languages, and consequently they enjoy a heightened "language sense" for the rest of their lives.

On most fields a family has more time to be together than do families in the homeland, where television has made its inroads and extracurricular and school activities prevent the family from having much time together.

The missionary child has early training in Christian service not enjoyed by most of his peers in the homeland. He also comes to feel early in life a personal responsibility for the spiritual well-being of others.

While it is perfectly true that housekeeping on the field is often more demanding in time and strength, the missionary wife finds great rewards in the area of homemaking. The sense of purpose and of dedication provide an atmosphere in which there are multiplied opportunities for meaningful, happy family living.

Not only this, but few Christians have the prayer help of

others to the extent that missionaries do. This is one of a missionary's greatest blessings.

Life on the mission field is so much easier than it was fifty or even twenty years ago that it is nearly impossible for most young missionary women to appreciate the difference, not having lived on the field during those earlier periods. Their lives would be sweetened with humility, gratefulness, and increased diligence if they could only conceive what their missionary forebears have taken in stride, for only one purpose—that Christ might be known. The automobile, the airplane, electricity, have changed the mode of living all over the world.

And then, of course, the supreme joy of missionary work is to see the living God work His miracle of grace in the lives of them who know Him not. This miracle is part of the outreach of the missionary's home, with a resulting fullness of joy that sheds its radiance over the whole life. It is no sacrifice to go to another land to see God work!

As to the major problem of balancing responsibilities, Dr. Henry Brandt, Christian psychologist, has written:

> I do not believe a missionary wife and mother is in a particularly unique position today. All over this world men and women both must choose what activities they will engage in. There is always more to do than one has time for and there are always decisions to be made whether one is going to try to keep up with all that is going on around him or be selective in what he chooses to do. It surely is true that conflict over family life would make a contribution to a nervous breakdown or emotional trouble. This would be true whether on the field or at home. Anyone is going to have emotional problems if he is indecisive about what he will, or will not, do. One of the standards that Paul sets for us is, "Whatsoever ye do, do it heartily as unto the Lord and not as unto men."
> . . . In an individual's life situation priorities will vary according to circumstances. At this point, you need to trust in the Lord to give you wisdom and the good judg-

ment you need in order to make reasonable decisions. Psalm 37:4, Proverbs16:3, Psalm 111:10, Psalm 112:5 are Bible verses which indicate that if we are rightly related to the Lord we can put faith in our judgments. When it comes to working together with other people, I Corinthians 1:10 is a criterion that should guide us in the judgments we make.[1]

It is the mother's own attitudes that count. Dr. Brandt has also written:

> The attitudes you give to your roles are also important, especially as they are impressed on your children. If you go at your work cheerfully and industriously, work to them will be a joy. If you are considerate of your inlaws, they will learn that this is the way to treat people.
>
> If you are a "church sleeper" or let work or golf or "week ending" come before the Lord's work, you can be sure that the value your son or daughter places on the church will be the same as they sense yours to be. This kind of behavior will almost certainly cancel out any high regard for the church you may have once planted in your children.
>
> And if by constant criticism you cut down the Christians with whom you work, in your role of churchman you will have utterly failed—no matter how busy you are for the Lord.[2]

In no sense is a missionary to be pitied, nor should a missionary mother ever feel sorry for herself or her children. While it is true that the spiritual warfare on the mission field is intense and that missionary work is done on enemy territory, we can only conclude that the problems a missionary mother faces are basically the same as those of any Christian mother.

The realization of this fact should help a missionary mother to slip down from her "unique" pedestal and examine her own work very critically.

[1]Personal letter from Dr. Henry Brandt, Dec. 26, 1963.
[2]Henry Brandt, Homer Dowdy, *Keep Your Roles in Balance.* Reprint in pamphlet form of an article in *Moody Monthly,* July-August, 1963, p. 9.

Is she being faithful as a mother? Do her children know the Lord? Are they being trained constantly and daily in the ways of the Lord? Is she preparing them for the years not far ahead when they will have to make their own choices and seek the Lord's will for themselves? Have they learned to accept hard things as coming from the Lord and for their own good?

Is she truly a missionary? Does she seek avenues of service or just accept what is imposed upon her? If her husband should be called to be with the Lord, would she no longer feel a responsibility to missionary work?

Granted that this must be a matter of personal guidance, it is still pertinent. Paul spoke searching, sobering words when, referring to the preaching of the Gospel, he said, "For if I do this thing willingly, I have a reward: but if against my will . . ." (I Cor. 9:17). Missionary women need to have burned deeply into them the spirit of "Woe is me if I preach not the Gospel!"

If a woman has this urge to make Christ known, all her life, however she is occupied, will be missionary life. Her every contact, whether in business or in friendliness with her neighbors, will be missionary in aim. The Lord will use her to reach people.

He will use her children as she seeks to reach people. But the conversation will not stop at the children; it will go on to the God who gave them, and who gave His own Son.

We would therefore present the following conclusions:

1. A woman's first and only responsibility is to fulfill the Lord's will for her, personally. This is ascertained in a daily walk with Him.

2. Her ministry can be greatly enlarged, under God's direction, by marriage and motherhood.

3. Since these relationships are from the hand of God, they do not conflict with missionary work given a mother; on the other hand, they do direct it along different channels for a period of years.

4. The peculiar responsibilities of child rearing occupy only a comparatively brief part of a missionary mother's time of service, while both she and the work benefit permanently from her years under the discipline of motherhood.

Christian . . . Wife . . . Mother . . . Missionary . . . Housewife?

If balancing your roles is important, so that no essential role is neglected, then does it not appear that the best measurement of your life is . . . the totality of your life—how you have brought every one of your roles with all its duties and responsibilities into obedience to the will of God?[3]

This, surely, is a worthy aim for the missionary mother.

---

[3]Brandt-Dowdy, *op. cit.,* p. 8.